Parents' Survival GUIDE TO I-75

Over **101** Fun Family Stops between Detroit & Orlando

Parents' Survival GUIDE TO I-75

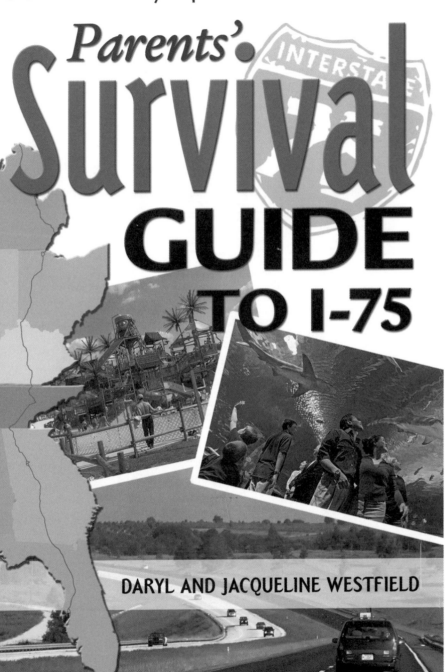

DARYL AND JACQUELINE WESTFIELD

Majestic Palm Press
Union, KY

The following trademarks appear throughout this book: AAA, TourBook, AARP, American Eagle, AZA, Belk, Burger King, Chick-Fil-A, Chuck E. Cheese, Coca-Cola, Coke, Dairy Queen, Dave & Buster's, Dillard's, Disney, Dunkin' Donuts, Elder-Beerman, Game Boy, Gatorland, Imagine It! The Children's Museum of Atlanta, Jay Jay The Jet Plane, JCPenney, Jillian's, KFC, Kroger, Kroger Plus, Macy's, Marshall Field's, Mayfield Dairy Farms, McDonald's, Nintendo, Parisian, Pizza Hut, A Place to Grow, Proffitt's, Sbarro, Sears, Six Flags Over Georgia, Starbucks, TCBY, Thomas the Tank Engine & Friends, TropiGrill, Victoria's Secret, Walt Disney World, Wendy's, Wild Adventures, Wild Waters Waterpark.

Although the authors have exhaustively researched all sources to ensure the accuracy and completeness of the information contained in this book, we assume no responsibility for errors, inaccuracies, omissions, or any other inconsistency herein. Prices and information in this book were verified at press time. We recommend, however, that you verify information before making final plans. Any slights against people or organizations are unintentional.

Exits with observed police or hospital signs are listed. The authors or publisher did not verify signed directions to the police stations or hospitals. Note that these police stations and hospitals may be many miles from I-75. Be sure to get local directions in an emergency.

Edited by PeopleSpeak
Cover & Interior design by Desktop Miracles, Inc.

Cover photos courtesy of the Newport Aquarium and Wild Adventures Amusement Park. Highway and minivan photos are from istockphoto.com.

Publisher's Cataloging-in-Publication Data

Westfield, Daryl.
    Parents' survival guide to I-75 : over 101 fun family stops between Detroit and Orlando / Daryl and Jacqueline Westfield.
       p.   cm.
    Includes index.
    ISBN 10: 1-933602-41-4 ISBN 13: 978-1-933602-41-7
    1. Family recreation.   2. Children—Travel—United States—Guidebooks.
3. Children—Travel—Michigan—Guidebooks.   4. Children—Travel—Ohio—Guidebooks.   5. Children—Travel—Tennessee—Guidebooks.
6. Children—Travel—Kentucky—Guidebooks.   7. Children—Travel—Georgia—Guidebooks.   8. Children—Travel—Florida—Guidebooks.   I. Westfield, Jacqueline.   II. Title.   III. Parents' survival guide to I-Seventy-Five : over a hundred-and-one fun family stops between Detroit and Orlando.
E158 .W47   2006
917.304—dc22   2005936829

Contents

Preface

Every year, thousands of families pack up their cars and drive along I-75 to visit friends, family, or a vacation destination. In fact, I-75 is a main corridor to Orlando, the most visited vacation area in the United States. While all family members look forward to their destination, many parents would agree that the drive there is quite often difficult and stressful. It doesn't have to be this way.

This book evolved from trips that our family has taken along I-75 to visit relatives in southern Florida and northern Ohio over more than 15 years. Early on, before we were blessed with our children, we would find places along I-75 to take driving breaks or to see something new. We enjoyed stopping at places such as museums, zoos, aquariums, and state parks. For our future reference, we took notes in a notebook. As the years passed, we gathered a pretty long list of fun places to visit. After we had children, new challenges arrived. What activities are fun for both kids and adults? Where can we stop for a potty break? What kinds of places are nearby where the kids can release some energy? We searched for a book that could help us answer these questions but couldn't find what we were looking for. This convinced us to write *Parents' Survival Guide to I-75*.

We conducted comprehensive research by reading, visiting Web sites, getting input from other families, and making numerous phone calls to find some additional great places along I-75. We have traveled thousands of miles visiting, reviewing, weeding out the not so good, and compiling the information.

Now, those who travel along I-75 anywhere between Detroit, Michigan, and Orlando, Florida, can use this book to explore the regions they drive through. We believe this book will help make any trip along I-75 more enjoyable.

Many thanks to our families for giving us reason to travel. Also special thanks to Mitchell and Alexandra for putting up with the extra stops Mom and Dad made along the way.

We sincerely hope you enjoy this book!

INTRODUCTION

Getting There

Who Can Benefit from This Book

Whether you are driving a short distance on I-75 to visit friends or family, traveling a major portion of I-75 to visit a theme park in Orlando, or heading to one of the cities along I-75, you can use *Parents' Survival Guide to I-75* as a road map to family fun.

This book gives you the information you need to enjoy any of the 27 museums, 7 zoos and aquariums, 35 parks (local, state, or national), 18 shopping malls, 16 family entertainment centers (Chuck E. Cheese, etc.), and almost 100 fast-food restaurants with indoor or outdoor play areas along I-75. We have included water parks, miniature golf courses, amusement parks, and any other fun family stop we could find. This book describes what activity is available, how long it takes to get there from I-75, detailed directions of the route driven by the authors, the age group that would enjoy the activity, the length of time you need to get the most from your visit, when the place is open, admission prices, and additional information you need to enjoy your visit. This book does not contain information about major theme parks in Orlando, which have been extensively written about in other travel books.

All of the activities are within 15 minutes of I-75, and most are just a few minutes away! Also, just in case of an emergency, we have included emergency phone numbers and listed exits with police or hospital signs visible from I-75.

How to Use This Book

This book is organized by state from north to south: it begins near Detroit, Michigan, and ends in Orlando, Florida. We have included a short trip on the Florida Turnpike, from the area south of Ocala to Orlando, as well as appropriate city bypass routes. In chapter 1, we give an attraction overview, organized by subject. For example, if you are looking for a children's museum and will be driving through southern Ohio, you can find Cinergy Children's Museum at Cincinnati Museum Center listed under "Children's Museums" with the appropriate I-75 exit numbers.

Chapters 2 through 7 are descriptions of activities located in each state along the drive. At the beginning of each state's chapter, we list "Top Family Stops," which are simply places that we enjoyed the most as a family. For quick reference, we also give a "Quick View" of the stops located in that particular state. Then, for each stop, the following information is described when applicable:

1. **Exit Number:** The exit that you take from I-75 to drive to the activity. If two exits are listed in the heading, the first number is the exit you take if you are driving south. The second number is the exit you take if you are heading north. See the driving directions under that particular stop for more details.

2. **Destination Name:** The name of the place to visit.

3. **Driving time:** The amount of time it took for the authors to drive from the interstate to the destination. If it took longer than 15 minutes for us to get to a destination, we didn't include it in the book.

4. **Ages:** The age range that will most enjoy the activity.

5. **Length of visit:** The amount of time you will probably need to get the most out of your visit.

6. **Address:** The physical address of the destination. You can use this to get directions from a Global Positioning System (GPS) if you have one in your vehicle.

7. **Directions:** Detailed driving directions that the authors used to travel to the destination. Be sure to ask for directions back to the highway if you are unsure. This is especially critical in major cities, such as Atlanta.

Lastly, most of I-75 runs close to north-south. The directions may say, "Take exit 111 and head west on XYZ Road" when in reality XYZ Road goes northwest or southwest at the exit. We found that saying "head west" is less confusing to the reader. "Head west" or "go west" means turning right from the highway if you are heading south on I-75 or turning left if you are heading north.

8. **Cost:** The price of admission and other costs, such as parking.
9. **Hours:** The operating hours of the destination.
10. **Phone:** The phone number of the destination.
11. **Web site:** The Web site to contact for further information. Many Web sites offer valuable coupons.
12. **Description and comments:** The authors' description of what is available to enjoy at the destination.

Great Ways to Save Money

The following are great money-saving tips that we use whenever traveling.

AAA

Use your AAA card for discounts to many of the activities listed in this book and to get better hotel rates. You can also call your local AAA office to get TripTiks that show you how to get to your destination and warn you of current construction projects. Finally, we always carry a AAA TourBook for the state we are driving through to get AAA-approved hotel information. AAA is our best traveling resource.

Kroger Plus Card

Show your Kroger Plus shopping card to get discounts to many attractions along I-75.

Hotels

You can save money on hotels if you stop at a rest area with tourist information and pick up a free copy of the green Traveler or red Travel Coupons book. These coupon books contain hotel coupons with highly discounted room rates. The coupons typically describe amenities and whether or not the hotel is AAA approved. We recommend staying at AAA approved hotels. Most of the time, the AAA approval rating is printed on the hotel coupon, but if not, you can refer to your AAA TourBook for that state to find the rating.

Another great way to save money on hotels is to reserve your room through the Internet via the hotel's Web site or an Internet travel service. The advantages to using this option are that you will get a good hotel rate plus you will be guaranteed a place to stay (we've all looked for a hotel late at night—no fun at all!). If you know what city you will be staying in but are unsure which hotel is best for you, visit http://www.tripadvisor.com/ before your trip to get reviews of hotels (we also reserve rooms directly through this site).

Our family enjoys an indoor pool to relax at in the evening as well as a free breakfast at the hotel so we can get a fast start on the drive. See appendix A for a listing of hotel chain toll-free numbers.

Memberships

Many museums, zoos, or aquariums are members of associations and may provide reciprocity. This means that one museum, zoo, or aquarium allows you free or discounted admission if you are a member of another museum, zoo, or aquarium in the same association. You may also be eligible for discounts in the museum stores. Use the following information if you want to find out more.

ASTC: Association of Science-Technology Centers Incorporated	(202) 783-7200	http://www.astc.org
AZA: The American Zoo and Aquarium Association	(301) 562-0777	http://www.aza.org
ACM: Association of Children's Museums	(202) 898-1080	http://www.childrens museums.org

AARP Discounts

Anyone over the age of 50 can join AARP and get discounts for hotels and many places listed in this book. Visit http://www.aarp.com/ for more information.

Web Coupons

Check out the Web sites listed in this book for applicable discounts or coupons. We have found substantial savings for theme parks on Internet Web sites.

Rest Areas and Hotel Lobbies

Visit rest areas and hotel lobbies for discount coupons to local attractions.

Disney Discounts

Be sure to visit http://www.mousesavers.com/ to find discounts on many items associated with Disney.

10 Tips for Arriving Refreshed

Many articles suggest you drive at night, especially when you have small children. We've never been good night drivers, so here are 10 survival tips to help you and your children pass the time on long car trips.

Plan Plenty of Stops

Using this book, of course, plan plenty of interesting or relaxing stops during the trip to break up the day. Most safety experts recommend stopping at least every two hours on long drives to rest the driver. Our driving day may look something like this:

6:00 a.m.	eat breakfast
7:00 a.m.	start driving
9:00 a.m.	take quick rest stop
11:30 a.m.	eat lunch at fast-food restaurant with play area
2:00 p.m.	take quick rest stop
4:30 p.m.	take longer stop at a park or other destination and eat dinner
8:00 p.m.	stop at hotel with pool

You can use this book to tailor the best plan for your family. It is filled with both special activities (museums, aquariums, zoos, etc.), where you might want to spend some quality time and those quick "let the kids run" stops.

Use the Standard Car Games You Grew Up With

Singing songs, playing I Spy, having scavenger hunts (make a list of things to look for out the window during the trip), and playing car license-plate games are still fun today. Our son started learning the 50 states by keeping track of license plates and marking them off on a map. Older kids may enjoy highlighting the travel route and calculating miles traveled or miles left to travel. Younger kids enjoy keeping track of the states through which you've traveled. See appendix B for more car game ideas.

Bring Lots of Snacks

We suggest you bring a combination of healthy snacks and those snacks that your kids love but typically don't eat at home. In our house, we don't eat a lot of high-sugar cereals. But we sometimes allow those little boxes of sugary delights during our long car trips and our kids love them. Try to avoid foods that need refrigeration or can melt in the sun or leave little hands sticky. Ideas for toddler snacks include finger foods, such as unsweetened cereal, whole grain crackers, graham crackers, cheese crackers, and ginger snaps. Avoid choking hazards like grapes, berries, raisins, nuts, dried fruit, and chunks of meat. Elementary-age kids can eat the toddler snacks plus items like fresh fruit, carrot or celery sticks, popcorn, and trail mixes. For teens, you may also want to include peanut butter sticks and energy bars. Our rule is that the kids can have a snack anytime they want one up to 30 minutes before a planned meal stop. It keeps them satisfied and happy. As long as we provide foods that are relatively healthy, we don't feel bad if their meals are eaten small snack by small snack throughout the day.

Pack a Small Cooler for Drinks

We pack a small, six-pack cooler with milk, water, clear fruit juice, and sodas. The small cooler provides easy in-and-out convenience in the front of the vehicle and allows us to keep a larger cooler (for items we may need in a day or two) closed. If you fill the small cooler with drinks that are already cold, just a few ice cubes will keep the drinks cold all day.

Buy a Few New Toys and Books for Each Child

Bring a bag of new toys and books for each of the children. As they get bored, pull a new surprise gift from the bag. Small books or magazines work well. So do travel-size games and magic eraser boards. Small, no-spill bubble containers are fun because kids think they are getting away with something while blowing bubbles in the car. Sticker books are also a hit. If you have older kids, make a trip to the library for some books before the trip (as long as you plan to return before they are due back).

Bring Their Favorite Music

Whether your children are old enough to use portable listening devices or they listen to CDs or tapes on the car stereo, music always helps soothe the savage child. Be sure to bring some grown-up music too. It's really nice when the kids start actually liking some of the music that you like. Our son was the first to sing Elvis and Beatles songs in his preschool class of 3-year-olds!

Bring a Personal Electronic Toy

It's hard to go anywhere without seeing school-age kids playing with their electronic toys (Game Boy, etc.). Friends of ours with older children think these are the greatest travel investments ever.

Check Out Some Books on Tape from the Library

Pick recorded stories that the whole family will enjoy. You'll be surprised how well they pass the time.

Get a Car Video Player

Whether you choose VHS or DVD, this device is the most valuable investment we can recommend to aid your drive. We bring tapes of the kids' favorite shows to help them pass the time. We certainly do not advocate watching videos all the time, but watching a few of their favorites along the way certainly helps smooth the trip.

Rotate through This List of Ideas

Every time your children get bored, try to suggest different activities from this list. Sometimes food will work, sometimes music. The key is to have so many tricks up your sleeve that you can always find something to help you pass that next thirty minutes of driving.

Please don't forget to buckle up! Have fun planning your trip!

Attraction Overview

Every family is different and so is every child. Maybe your child is a history buff or a budding scientist. Or maybe your child would have the most fun at a park where he or she can climb, slide, and swing. In this chapter, we have grouped fun family stops into subjects to help you plan your trip.

Science

What	Where
The New Detroit Science Center	MI Exit 53A
COSI Toledo	OH Exit 202A/201B
Armstrong Air & Space Museum	OH Exit 111
National Museum of the United States Air Force	OH Exit 58/54C
Boonshoft Museum of Discovery	OH Exit 57B
Museum of Natural History & Science at Cincinnati Museum Center	OH Exit 2A/1G
East Tennessee Discovery Center	TN Exit 107A/ I-40 East
The Lost Sea	TN Exit 60
Mayfield Dairy Farms	TN Exit 52
Creative Discovery Museum	TN Exit 2
Weinman Mineral Museum	GA Exit 293
The Museum of Arts and Sciences	GA Exit 9 (I-475)
Florida Museum of Natural History	FL Exit 384
Orlando Science Center	FL Turnpike Exit 265

Sports

What	Where
The Cincinnati Reds Hall of Fame and Museum	OH Exit 1A
World of Sports	KY Exit 181
Florence/Boone County State Park	KY Exit 181
Sports of All Sorts	KY Exits 181, 178
Kentucky Horse Park	KY Exit 120
Galaxy Bowling Center	KY Exit 87
Putt-Putt Golf & Games	TN Exit 373 (I-40/I-75)
Don Garlits Museum of Drag Racing	FL Exit 341

Children's Museums

What	Where
COSI Toledo	OH Exit 202A/201B
Boonshoft Museum of Discovery	OH Exit 57B
Cinergy Children's Museum at Cincinnati Museum Center	OH Exit 2A/1G
Totter's Otterville at Johnny's Toys	KY Exit 185
Explorium of Lexington	KY Exit 113
East Tennessee Discovery Center	TN Exit 107A/ I-40 East
Creative Discovery Museum	TN Exit 2
Imagine It! The Children's Museum of Atlanta	GA Exit 249C/248C
The Museum of Arts and Sciences	GA Exit 9 (I-475)
Orlando Science Center	FL Turnpike Exit 265

Parks and Playgrounds

What	Where
Belle Isle Park	MI Exit 51
Lake Erie MetroPark	MI Exit 29A
Sterling State Park	MI Exit 15
Van Buren State Park	OH Exit 164
Botkins Community Park	OH Exit 104
Highfield Discovery Garden	OH Exit 14
Sawyer Point Park	OH Exit 1A
Crescent Springs Community Park	KY Exit 186
Stringtown Park	KY Exit 181
South Fork Park	KY Exit 180
Ockerman Park	KY Exit 180
Big Bone Lick State Park	KY Exit 175
Walton City Park	KY Exit 171
Kentucky Horse Park	KY Exit 120
Fort Boonesborough State Park	KY Exit 95
Levi Jackson Wilderness Road State Park	KY Exit 38
Indian Mountain State Park	TN Exit 160
Cove Lake State Park	TN Exit 134

Parks and Playgrounds (cont'd)

What	Where
Norris Dam State Park	TN Exit 128
Campbell Station Park	TN Exit 373
	(I-40/I-75)
Athens Regional Park	TN Exit 49
Chickamauga Battlefield National Military Park	GA Exit 350
Red Top Mountain State Park	GA Exit 285
Kennesaw Mountain National Battlefield Park	GA Exit 269
Piedmont Park	GA Exit 250
Centennial Olympic Park	GA Exit 249C/248C
High Falls State Park	GA Exit 198
Fulwood Park	GA Exit 63A
Reed Bingham State Park	GA Exit 39
Stephen Foster Folk Culture Center State Park	FL Exit 439
O'Leno State Park	FL Exit 414
Paynes Prairie Preserve State Park	FL Exit 374

Nature and Animals

What	Where
Detroit Zoo	MI Exit 61
Lake Erie MetroPark	MI Exit 29A
Sterling State Park	MI Exit 15
Toledo Zoo	OH Exit 201A
Cox Arboretum MetroPark	OH Exit 44
Highfield Discovery Garden	OH Exit 14
Cincinnati Zoo & Botanical Garden	OH Exit 6
Newport Aquarium	KY Exit 192
Big Bone Lick State Park	KY Exit 175
Kentucky Horse Park	KY Exit 120
Fort Boonesborough State Park	KY Exit 95
Levi Jackson Wilderness Road State Park	KY Exit 38
Indian Mountain State Park	TN Exit 160
Cove Lake State Park	TN Exit 134
Norris Dam State Park	TN Exit 128

Nature and Animals (cont'd)

What	Where
The Museum of Appalachia	TN Exit 122
Knoxville Zoo	TN Exit 107A/ I-40 East
Tennessee Aquarium	TN Exit 2
Chickamauga Battlefield National Military Park	GA Exit 350
Etowah Indian Mounds Historic Site	GA Exit 288
Red Top Mountain State Park	GA Exit 285
Kennesaw Mountain National Battlefield Park	GA Exit 269
Piedmont Park	GA Exit 250
Zoo Atlanta	GA Exit 247
High Falls State Park	GA Exit 198
Georgia Agrirama	GA Exit 63B
Paradise Public Fishing Area	GA Exit 62
Reed Bingham State Park	GA Exit 39
Stephen Foster Folk Culture Center State Park	FL Exit 439
O'Leno State Park	FL Exit 414
Paynes Prairie Preserve State Park	FL Exit 374
Gatorland	FL Turnpike Exit 254

History

What	Where
Motown Historical Museum	MI Exit 54/49B
Charles H. Wright Museum of African American History	MI Exit 53A
Detroit Historical Museum	MI Exit 53A
River Raisin Battlefield Visitor Center	MI Exit 14
Armstrong Air & Space Museum	OH Exit 111
National Museum of the United States Air Force	OH Exit 58/54C
Cincinnati History Museum at Cincinnati Museum Center	OH Exit 2A/1G
Cincinnati Fire Museum	OH Exit 1C
National Underground Railroad Freedom Center	OH Exit 1A
Fort Boonesborough State Park	KY Exit 95

History (cont'd)

What	Where
KFC Museum	KY Exit 29
The Museum of Appalachia	TN Exit 122
Chickamauga Battlefield National Military Park	GA Exit 350
Etowah Indian Mounds Historic Site	GA Exit 288
Southern Museum of Civil War and Locomotive History	GA Exit 273
Kennesaw Mountain National Battlefield Park	GA Exit 269
World of Coca-Cola	GA Exit 248A/246
Georgia Agrirama	GA Exit 63B
Stephen Foster Folk Culture Center State Park	FL Exit 439
Florida Museum of Natural History	FL Exit 384

Shopping Malls

What	Where
Oakland Mall	MI Exit 65A
Miami Valley Centre Mall	OH Exit 82
Dayton Mall	OH Exit 44
Tri-County Mall	OH Exit 16
Cincinnati Mills Mall	OH Exit 16
Newport on the Levee	KY Exit 192
Florence Mall	KY Exit 180A/180
West Town Mall	TN Exit 380 (I-40/I-75)
Hamilton Place Mall	TN Exit 5/4A
Town Center at Cobb Mall	GA Exit 269
Cumberland Mall	GA Exit 258
Southlake Mall	GA Exit 233
Colonial Mall Macon	GA Exit 5 (I-475)
Colonial Mall Valdosta	GA Exit 18
Lake City Mall	FL Exit 427
The Oaks Mall	FL Exit 387
Paddock Mall	FL Exit 350
West Oaks Mall	FL Turnpike Exit 267B

Water Parks and Amusement Parks

What	Where
Chandler Park Family Aquatic Center	MI Exit 53B
Florence Aquatic Center	KY Exit 181
Hal Rogers Family Entertainment Center/ Kentucky Splash Water Park	KY Exit 11
American Adventures	GA Exit 265
Six Flags White Water	GA Exit 265
Six Flags Over Georgia	GA Exit 10B (I-285)
Wild Adventures	GA Exit 13
Wild Waters Waterpark	FL Exit 352

Family Entertainment Centers

What	Where
Dave & Buster's	OH Exit 16
Jillian's	KY Exit 191
Sports of All Sorts	KY Exit 181
Chuck E. Cheese	KY Exit 180A/180
Sports of All Sorts	KY Exit 178
Chuck E. Cheese	KY Exit 110
Hal Rogers Family Entertainment Center/ Kentucky Splash Water Park	KY Exit 11
Chuck E. Cheese	TN Exit 379A/379 (I-40/I-75)
Zuma Fun Center	TN Exit 378 (I-40/I-75)
Putt-Putt Golf & Games	TN Exit 373 (I-40/I-75)
Chuck E. Cheese	GA Exit 269
Dave & Buster's	GA Exit 261
Chuck E. Cheese	GA Exits 258/ 5 (I-475)
Olympia Family Fun Center	GA Exit 5 (I-475)
Chuck E. Cheese	FL Turnpike Exit 267B

Michigan

Saginaw

75

Flint

96

96

69

94

196

Pontiac

★ Lansing

Troy

96

Kalamazoo

94

275

Detroit

94

Ann Arbor

94

69

75

Top Michigan Family Stops

Detroit Zoo
Charles H. Wright Museum of African American History
The New Detroit Science Center
Lake Erie MetroPark

Michigan Quick View

Attraction	Michigan Exit Number
Zoo or Aquarium	61
Park	51, 29A, 15
Museum	54/49B, 53A, 14
Mall	65A
Family Entertainment Center	None
Rest Area Mile Marker	10 (northbound only)
Fast Food with an Indoor Play Area	11
Fast Food with an Outdoor Play Area	None
Other Attraction	53B

Michigan Emergency Information

Emergency Phone:	911
Michigan State Police Headquarters:	(517) 332-2521
Exit with Police Sign:	11
Exits with Hospital Sign:	55, 29A, 15

Exit 65A

Oakland Mall

Driving time:	3 minutes
Ages:	2 and up
Length of visit:	1 hour
Address:	412 West 14 Mile Road, Troy, MI 48083
Directions:	Take exit 65A (14 Mile Road East) and go east 0.2 mile. The Oakland Mall is on the left.
Cost:	Free
Hours:	Mon–Sat 10 a.m.–9 p.m., Sun 11 a.m.–6 p.m.
Phone:	(248) 585–6000
Web site:	http://www.oaklandmall.com
Description and comments:	This major mall offers over 180 stores and restaurants, including Sears, JCPenney, and Marshall Field's. Visit the food court, which includes pizza, subs, and Chinese food. Kids can enjoy the arcade on the upper floor near JCPenney. Youngsters under the age of 6 can crawl and play on the animal-themed soft play area on the lower floor near JCPenney.

Interstate Information

One- or two-digit *even-numbered* interstates are always east-west routes. The numbers increase from the south (I-4) to the north (I-96).

One- or two-digit *odd-numbered* interstates are always north-south routes. The numbers increase from the West Coast (I-5) to the East Coast (I-95).

Mile-marker numbers begin counting at a state's southern border (for north-south routes). Knowing exactly where you are with reference to a mile marker can be a big help when you plan your next stop or ask for roadside assistance in an emergency.

Exit 61

Detroit Zoo

Driving time:	4 minutes
Ages:	All
Length of visit:	3 hours
Address:	8450 West 10 Mile Road, Royal Oak, MI 48068
Directions:	Take exit 61 (I-696 west) and head west 1.5 miles. Take I-696 exit 16 (Woodward Avenue/Main Street) and go straight 0.7 mile. The Detroit Zoo entrance is on the right.
Cost:	$11 adults $9 seniors (ages 62 and up) $7 children (ages 2–12) Free for children under 2 Parking: $5 Simulator rides: $4 One-way miniature train rides: $2 This zoo is a member of AZA.
Hours:	November–March, Wed–Sun 10 a.m.–4 p.m. April–June, daily 10 a.m.–5 p.m. July and August, Thu–Tue 10 a.m.–5 p.m., Wed 10 a.m.–8 p.m. September and October, daily 10 a.m.–5 p.m. The miniature railroad operates daily May–September and weekends in October.
Phone:	(248) 398–0900
Web site:	http://www.detroitzoo.org/
Description and comments:	It was another warm and steamy 78-degree January day in Detroit, Michigan. Did I forget to mention that we were in the aviary at the Detroit Zoo? Perhaps you would prefer the frozen tundra at the Arctic Ring of Life, the largest polar bear

exhibit in the world. Here you can view polar bears in their natural habitat, walk through a tunnel surrounded by swimming seals, and visit an arctic exploration station. Bears, primates, giraffes, elephants, reptiles, and amphibians round out the assortment of animals at this zoo. Kids will enjoy the large outdoor playgrounds (one area for those aged 2–5 and one for those aged 5–12) and riding the train from one end of the zoo to the other. Wild Adventure Simulator rides allow those over 36 inches tall to experience Seeing the World Through the Eyes of the Animals or take a submersible journey into the Deep Sea.

Exit 54 or 49B

Motown Historical Museum

Driving time:	7 minutes
Ages:	8 and up
Length of visit:	1 hour
Address:	2648 West Grand Boulevard, Detroit, MI 48208
Directions heading south:	Take exit 54 (East Grand Boulevard/Clay Avenue) and go straight off the exit 0.2 mile. Turn right on East Grand Boulevard and go 2 miles. The museum is on the left.
Directions heading north:	Take exit 49B (MI-10 north John C. Lodge Expressway) and head north 2 miles. Take the MI-10 West Grand Boulevard exit. Turn left on West Grand Boulevard and go 0.3 mile. The museum is on the left.
Cost:	$8 adults $5 children (ages 12 and younger)
Hours:	Tue–Sat 10 a.m.–6 p.m.
Phone:	(313) 875-2264

Web site:	http://www.motownmuseum.com/
Description and comments:	Stop and see memorabilia that traces the history of Motown music. Visit Studio A and see the original instruments and equipment used during recording sessions of greats such as Marvin Gaye, Stevie Wonder, the Temptations, the Four Tops, Gladys Knight and the Pips, and the Jackson Five. You can even find Michael Jackson's famous rhinestone glove on display.

Exit 53B

Chandler Park Family Aquatic Center

Driving time:	9 minutes
Ages:	All
Length of visit:	3 hours
Address:	12600 Chandler Park Drive, Detroit, MI 48213
Directions:	Take exit 53B (I-94 east) and head east 4 miles. Take I-94 exit 220B (Conner Avenue) and veer right on Conner Avenue. Go south 0.3 mile. Chandler Park is on the left.
Cost:	Park: Free
	Aquatic Center: Mon–Fri $6 adults $4 children (ages 2–16) Free for children under 2
	Weekends $7 adults $5 children (ages 2–16) Free for children under 2
Hours:	Park: Dawn–dusk

Aquatic Center:
Memorial Day–late June, Weekends 10 a.m.–8 p.m.

Late June–Labor Day, Mon–Fri 11 a.m.–8 p.m.,
Weekends and holidays 10 a.m.–8 p.m.

Phone: (888) 995-7665

Web site: http://www.chandlerpark.com/

Description and Chandler Park is a community park with plenty
comments: of green space where you can enjoy the outdoors.
                     Kids can play on the outdoor baseball diamond
                     and basketball courts or visit the aquatic center
                     on a hot summer day. At the aquatic center, take
                     a plunge down the water slides, float in the wave
                     pool, and let the kids play in the children's activ-
                     ity pool. If you get hungry, you can get pizza,
                     burgers, hot dogs, and ice cream at the conces-
                     sions area. Restrooms are available.

EXIT

Exit 53A

Charles H. Wright Museum of African American History
The New Detroit Science Center
Detroit Historical Museum

Charles H. Wright Museum of African American History

Driving time: 3 minutes

Ages: 8 and up

Length of visit: 2 hours

Address: 315 East Warren Avenue, Detroit, MI 48201

Directions: Take exit 53A (Warren Avenue) and go west 0.3
                     mile. Turn right on Brush Street. Go 1 block and
                     turn left on Farnsworth Street. Go 1 block and
                     turn left on John R. Street. Parking for both the
                     Museum of African American History and the
                     New Detroit Science Center is on the left.

Cost:	$8 adults
	$5 seniors (ages 62 and up)
	$5 children (ages 3–12)
	Free for children under 3
	Parking: $5 in the museum lot
Hours:	Wed–Thu 9:30 a.m.–3 p.m.,
	Fri–Sat 9:30 a.m.–5 p.m.
Phone:	(313) 494–5800
Web site:	http://www.maah-detroit.org/
Description and comments:	The permanent exhibit And Still We Rise is a journey through African American history and culture. The story begins in Africa over 3.5 million years ago and ends in modern Detroit. Visitors can walk through a slaveholding area as well as a slave ship, complete with realistic moaning sounds of the slaves in their decrepit ship's quarters. This museum also houses many temporary cultural and historical African American exhibits. This is a great place for anyone who wants to learn more about African American history.

The New Detroit Science Center

Driving time:	3 minutes
Ages:	3 and up
Length of visit:	2 hours
Address:	5020 John R. Street, Detroit, MI 48202
Directions:	Take exit 53A (Warren Avenue) and go west 0.3 mile. Turn right on Brush Street. Go 1 block and turn left on Farnsworth Street. Go 1 block and turn left on John R. Street. Parking for both the Museum of African American History and the New Detroit Science Center is on the left.

Cost:	$7 adults
	$6 seniors (ages 60 and up)
	$6 children (ages 2–12)
	Free for children under 2
	Parking: $5 in the museum lot
	IMAX movies: $4
	This museum is a member of ASTC.
Hours:	Day after Labor Day–mid-June, Mon–Fri 9 a.m.–3 p.m., Sat 10:30 p.m.–6 p.m., Sun noon–6 p.m.
	Mid-June–Labor Day, Mon–Fri 9 a.m.–5 p.m., Sat 10:30 a.m.–6 p.m., Sun noon–6 p.m.
Phone:	(313) 577-8400
Web site:	http://www.sciencedetroit.org/
Description and comments:	There's a lot of science to be learned in the New Detroit Science Center. This museum, which re-opened in 2001, has something for all budding scientists. In the Motion Lab, kids love to pull themselves up with a pulley chair, lift heavy objects with levers, and spin things really fast with gears. Downstairs at the Life Sciences Lab, kids

Photo courtesy of the New Detroit Science Center

can learn about waves and vibration (with a musical instrument "jam room") and electricity. The electrical demonstrations at Sparks Theater are very popular with the kids. The SBC Children's Gallery is a special science area just for those aged 6 and under. Here, younger children can build with blocks, play with water, and put on puppet shows. Complete your visit with a trip to the café, which serves hot food and sandwiches.

Detroit Historical Museum

Driving time:	4 minutes
Ages:	8 and up
Length of visit:	3 hours
Address:	5401 Woodward Avenue, Detroit, MI 48202
Directions:	Take exit 53A (Warren Avenue) and go west 0.6 mile. Turn right on Woodward Avenue. Go 2 blocks and turn left on Kirby Street West. Detroit Historical Museum parking is on the right.
Cost:	$5 adults $3 seniors (ages 60 and up) $3 children (ages 5–18) Free for children under 5 Wednesday admission is $2.50 for all visitors. Parking: $3 weekdays Free weekends in the limited museum lot Metered lots are available in the area. This museum does not take credit cards.
Hours:	Wed–Fri 9:30 a.m.–3 p.m., Sat 10 a.m.–5 p.m., Sun noon–5 p.m. Closed Christmas Eve, Christmas Day, and New Year's Day.
Phone:	(313) 833–1805
Web site:	http://www.detroithistorical.org/

Description and comments:	Take a walk through the Streets of Old Detroit where you will find replicas of shops from the 1840s to 1900. The Motor City is an interesting exhibit where you can see the impact of the automotive industry on Detroit. We enjoyed watching the car assembly line and seeing the "body drop" in action. Kids enjoy viewing the Glancy Trains exhibit, where small-scale trains abound. You can also learn about Detroit's role in the Underground Railroad at the Doorway to Freedom. This is definitely the place to go if you want to learn about the history of Detroit.

Exit 51

Belle Isle Park

Driving time:	7 minutes
Ages:	2 and up
Length of visit:	3 hours
Address:	100 Strand Drive, Belle Isle, Detroit, MI 48207
Directions:	Take exit 51 (I-375 South/Downtown) and go south 0.5 mile. Take the I-375 Jefferson Avenue East exit and go 2 miles. Turn right at East Grand Boulevard. Go across the Douglas Macarthur Bridge to Belle Isle Park.
Cost:	Park and conservatory: Free Dossin Great Lakes Museum: $3.50 adults $2.50 seniors (ages 62 and up) $2.50 children (ages 4–18) Free for children under 4 Water slides: $3
Hours:	Park: Dawn–dusk Conservatory: 10 a.m.–5 p.m. Dossin Great Lakes Museum: Sat–Sun 11 a.m.–5 p.m.

Water slides:
Memorial Day–Labor Day, daily noon–7:45 p.m.

Phone: Belle Isle Park: (313) 852–4075
                         Dossin Great Lakes Museum: (313) 852–4051

Web site: http://www.fobi.org/
                         http://www.detroithistorical.org/

Description and   Belle Isle Park is a 2.5-mile-long island in the
comments: middle of the Detroit River. Once you cross the
                         bridge to the island, take a drive around the
                         perimeter and you will find fishing piers, soccer
                         fields, multiple playgrounds, water slides, baseball
                         fields, and a golf driving range. Our favorite activ-
                         ity was walking along the shoreline and watching
                         the geese and other waterfowl. Also within the
                         park is the Dossin Great Lakes Museum, where
                         you can learn about the shipping industry of the
                         Great Lakes and the ecology of the Detroit River.
                         Also, be sure to check out the free conservatory,
                         where you will find a great display of tropical and
                         desert flora. This is truly a unique experience,
                         only minutes from downtown Detroit.

Check out the Marathon Oil tank near the west side of MI exit 43. It
commemorates both the Detroit Pistons' and the Detroit Shock's
recent championships.

Exit 29A

Lake Erie MetroPark

Driving time: 7 minutes

Ages: 3 and up

Length of visit: 2 hours

Address: 32481 West Jefferson Avenue
                         Brownstown, MI 48173

Directions:	Take exit 29A (Gibraltar Road) and head east 2 miles. Turn right on West Jefferson Avenue and go 1.5 miles. Lake Erie MetroPark is on the left. Directions are signed from I-75.
Cost:	$4 per vehicle Wave pool: $4 adults $3.50 seniors (ages 62 and up) $3.50 children (ages 15 and younger)
Hours:	Park: 6 a.m.–10 p.m. Wave pool: Memorial Day weekend–Labor Day Daily 10 a.m.–8 p.m. (hours may be reduced from mid-August to Labor Day) Marshlands Museum and Nature Center: Mon–Fri 1 p.m.–5 p.m., Weekends 10 a.m.–5 p.m.
Phone:	(734) 379–5020
Web site:	http://www.metroparks.com/
Description and comments:	The Lake Erie MetroPark is a 1,607-acre recreational facility that has something for everyone. The 3-mile shoreline view along the banks of Lake Erie is a great place for bird-watching and viewing other wildlife that inhabit the lagoons and marshes. You can borrow a free fishing pole and try your luck from the bank. Children aged 3–10 will enjoy the large outdoor playground (follow signs to the "tot lot"), which features slides, swings, bridges, and a lighthouse. Marshlands Museum and Nature Center features a 1,300-gallon aquarium that showcases regional fish species. From the museum area, you can take a picturesque walk along several miles of walking trails. On a hot summer day, be sure to bring your bathing suits and try the Great Wave pool, complete with 3-foot waves.

Exit 15

Sterling State Park

Driving time:	3 minutes
Ages:	2 and up
Length of visit:	2 hours
Address:	2800 State Park Road, Monroe, MI 48162
Directions:	Take exit 15 (MI-50/Dixie Highway) and go east 0.8 mile. Sterling State Park is on the right.
Cost:	$8 per nonresident vehicle $6 per Michigan resident vehicle
Hours:	Early April–December, 8 a.m.–dusk Memorial Day–Labor Day, 8 a.m.–10 p.m. Call for winter or spring hours (the park closes after the first heavy frost because some of the dirt roads become impassible).
Phone:	(734) 289-2715
Web site:	http://www.michigandnr.com/parksandtrails/ Click on Search.
Description and comments:	Located on the shores of Lake Erie, Sterling State Park is a 1,000-acre recreational area. This is a great place to view migratory birds in the fall as well as other wildlife and plants that inhabit the shores of Lake Erie. Try your luck shore fishing at one of the lagoons or fishing piers. Take a walk along the 6 miles of trails, or bring a picnic and relax along the 1-mile sandy beach on Lake Erie. Kids love the playground with a solid rubber surface. Vending machines, restrooms, grills, and picnic tables are available.

Michigan Trivia

· The word *Michigan* is from the Chippewa word *Michigama*, meaning "great lake."

· Michigan became the 26th state in 1837.

· Lansing became the capital in 1847.

· The first auto traffic tunnel built between two nations was the mile-long Detroit-Windsor tunnel under the Detroit River.

· Detroit is known as the car capital of the world.

· Michigan has the longest freshwater shoreline in the world.

Exit 14

River Raisin Battlefield Visitor Center

Driving time:	2 minutes
Ages:	8 and up
Length of visit:	1 hour
Address:	1403 East Elm Avenue, Monroe, MI 48162
Directions:	Take exit 14 (Elm Avenue) and go west 0.4 mile. River Raisin Battlefield Visitor Center is on the right.
Cost:	Free (donations are appreciated)
Hours:	June–August, Fri–Tue, 10 a.m.–5 p.m.
	September, October, January, April, May, Weekends only, 10 a.m.–5 p.m.
	Closed November, December, February, March.
Phone:	(734) 243-7136
Web site:	http://www.co.monroe.mi.us/ Under government, click on Departments, click on Museum, then click on River Raisin Battlefield.

Description and comments:	The River Raisin Battlefield Visitor Center contains exhibits from the Battle of the River Raisin during the War of 1812. The battle was fought at this site on January 22, 1813. Almost all of the 934 Americans who fought here were captured or killed. The museum includes clothing from British and American soldiers, pottery and artifacts found near the site, and a fiber-optic map showing details of the battle.

Exit 11

McDonald's with an Indoor Play Area

Driving time:	1 minute
Directions:	Take exit 11 (LaPlaisance Road/Downtown Monroe) and go west 0.4 mile. McDonald's is on the right.

Michigan Mile Marker 10

Michigan Welcome Center (*northbound only*)

The visitor information booth is open 9 a.m.–9 p.m. in the summer and 9 a.m.–5 p.m. the remainder of the year. Restrooms are always available.

THREE

Ohio

Top Ohio Family Stops

COSI Toledo

Toledo Zoo

National Museum of the United States Air Force

Boonshoft Museum of Discovery

Cincinnati Zoo & Botanical Garden

Cincinnati Museum Center at Union Terminal

Ohio Quick View

Attraction	Ohio Exit Number
Zoo or Aquarium	201A, 6
Park	164, 104, 44, 14, 1A
Museum	202A/201B, 111, 58/54C, 57B, 2A/1G, 1C, 1A
Mall	82, 44, 16
Family Entertainment Center	16
Rest Area Mile Marker	179, 153, 114, 80, 28
Fast Food with an Indoor Play Area	68, 63
Fast Food with an Outdoor Play Area	142, 92 82, 74, 22
Other Attraction	None

Ohio Emergency Information

Emergency Phone:	911
Ohio Highway Patrol (from Ohio only):	(877) 772–8765
Exits with Police Sign:	161, 124, 111, 110, 82, 60
Exits with Hospital Sign:	203A, 181, 156, 140, 125, 82, 78, 74, 73, 54B, 51, 44, 32

Exit 202A or 201B

COSI Toledo (Center of Science and Industry)

Driving time:	5 minutes
Ages:	All
Length of visit:	2–4 hours
Address:	One Discovery Way, Toledo, OH 43604
Directions heading south:	Take exit 202A (Toledo/South Washington Street/Downtown) and go south on Washington Street 0.5 mile. Turn left on Summit Street and go 0.5 mile. COSI is on the right. Follow signs to any of the nearby parking lots. Directions to COSI are marked from I-75.
Directions heading north:	Take exit 201B (25N/Downtown), turn left on Erie Street, and go 0.1 mile. Turn right on Washington Street and go 0.2 mile. Turn left on Summit Street and go 0.5 mile. COSI is on the right. Follow signs to any of the nearby parking lots. Directions to COSI are marked from I-75.
Cost:	$8.50 adults $7.50 seniors (ages 65 and up) $6.50 children (ages 3–12) Free for children under 3 Parking: $2 with a COSI validation stamp in local garages This museum is a member of ASTC and ACM.
Hours:	Mon–Sat 10 a.m.–5 p.m., Sun noon–5 p.m. Closed New Year's Day, Easter, Thanksgiving Day, Christmas Eve, and Christmas Day.
Phone:	(800) 334-2674
Web site:	http://www.cositoledo.org/

Description and comments: Kids of all ages will enjoy a couple of hours, or all day, at this science center. At COSI Toledo there are many "Learning Worlds." At Whiz Bang Engineering you can ride in a hydraulic motion simulator or build a bridge and test its strength. Sports is a kid favorite. This area features activities such as a virtual volleyball game and rock climbing. Kids especially like to measure how high they can jump and how fast they can run or throw a ball. Water Works is a great place to play in and learn about water. It includes sand areas and a miniature submarine to enjoy. Be sure to bring some dry clothes if you and your family plan to play in this area. Little KIDSPACE is a good spot for kindergarteners and younger, with a miniature water play area and a pretend ambulance. Our kids liked to bang on many common items with a drumstick to hear what noises they made. Mindzone is full of optical illusions, some of which are so strong you can get dizzy. This area is probably best for older kids and adults.

Learning about rats (Photo courtesy of COSI Toledo)

Our kids liked the activities outside the "Worlds" the best. They enjoyed filling two hot-air balloons and seeing which went higher or faster. The perpetual-motion ball display was mesmerizing. This display is made of pool-table balls that roll down a series of obstacles until reaching the bottom, making a lot of noise as they hit chimes and other noisemakers on the way down.

Eat at the Atomic Café or at the H2O Patio (open Memorial Day–Labor Day). Shop for unique toys and activities at Science 2 Go.

Exit 201A

Toledo Zoo

Driving time:	5 minutes
Ages:	All
Length of visit:	2–4 hours
Address:	2700 Broadway, Toledo, OH 43609
Directions:	Take exit 201A (to OH-25S/Collingwood) and head west off the exit. Go 3 miles southwest on OH-25 to the Toledo Zoo parking lot.
Cost:	$9 adults $6 seniors (ages 60 and up) $6 children (ages 2–11) Free to children under 2 Parking: $5 Train ride: $2 Free for children under 2 Africa! carousel: $1.50 Historic carousel: $1 This zoo is a member of AZA.

Hours:	May–Labor Day 10 a.m.–5 p.m.
	Labor Day–April 10 a.m.–4 p.m.
	The children's zoo, carousels, and Africa! train ride are open Memorial Day–Labor Day.
	Closed Thanksgiving Day, Christmas Day, and New Year's Day.
Phone:	(419) 385-5721
Web site:	http://www.toledozoo.org/
Description and comments:	Rated as one of the top 10 zoos in the country by a leading children's magazine, the Toledo Zoo is a great stop for families. Enjoy over 700 species of animals, with exhibits including an aviary, wolves, apes, an aquarium, a museum of science, a children's zoo, and a hippoquarium, where hippos can be seen underwater. The many interesting indoor exhibits make this a good trip even when the weather is not cooperating. The zoo opened Africa! in May 2004. Zebras, impalas, giraffes, and ostriches roam the plains. A safari train circles the 10-acre exhibit and a carousel features African animals. Toddlers and preschoolers will enjoy the outdoor playground. Our family especially enjoyed the aquarium. The native Ohio fish and the coral reef tanks are very well done. The Siberian tigers are also impressive. Wagons or strollers can be rented at the zoo.

Ohio Trivia

- Ohio is known as the "Mother of Presidents." Seven United States presidents were born in Ohio: Ulysses S. Grant, Rutherford B. Hayes, James A. Garfield, Benjamin Harrison, William McKinley, William H. Taft, and Warren G. Harding. William Henry Harrison, who was born in Virginia but settled in Ohio, is also claimed as one of Ohio's own.

- Ohio became the 17th state in 1803.

- Ohio ranks number one in the country for egg and Swiss cheese production.

Ohio Mile Marker 179

Ohio Welcome Center

This rest area has tourist information, restrooms, vending machines, picnic tables, and space for kids to run. Be sure to pick up a free coupon book if you are planning to stop at a hotel in Ohio.

Exit 164

Van Buren State Park

Driving time:	3 minutes
Ages:	All
Length of visit:	1–3 hours
Address:	12259 Township Road 218 Van Buren, OH 45889
Directions:	Take exit 164 (OH-613/Fostoria/McComb) and go east 0.8 mile. Turn right (immediately after the railroad tracks) on Township Road 218 to Van Buren State Park.
Cost:	Free
Hours:	Dawn–dusk
Phone:	(419) 832-7662
Web site:	http://www.ohiodnr.com/parks/
Description and comments:	Named after the eighth president of the United States, the serene Van Buren State Park is just a few minutes from I-75. Enjoy fishing or boating (no gas motors) on the 45-acre lake. Largemouth bass, bluegills, channel catfish, crappie, and carp inhabit the lake. There are unpaved hiking trails around the lake, as well as 6 miles of multiuse trails. You can also enjoy volleyball courts, non-electric campsites, picnic areas, and horseshoe pits. Plenty of space is available for kids to run around on a sunny afternoon.

Kid Trivia

Findlay, Ohio, calls itself "Flag City USA." Check out the mural on the Marathon Oil tank near mile marker 157.

Ohio Mile Marker 153

Rest Area

This rest area has restrooms, telephones, vending machines, picnic tables, and space for kids to run.

Exit 142

McDonald's with an Outdoor Play Area

Driving time: 1 minute

Directions: Take exit 142 (OH-103/Arlington/Bluffton) and go west 0.3 mile. McDonald's is on the right.

Description: The outdoor playground has five slides and a bridge. There is a Lego table inside the restaurant large enough for two kids to play.

Looking for a Hotel?

During a January snowstorm, we took refuge at the Bluffton Comfort Inn, just west of I-75 at OH exit 142. For under $80, we received a nice room with a queen bed, access to a heated indoor pool, and a continental breakfast. This hotel is a three (out of five) diamond AAA-rated hotel. Call (419) 358–6000 to speak to the hotel staff.

Ohio Mile Marker 114

Rest Area

This rest area has restrooms, telephones, vending machines, picnic tables, and space for kids to run.

Exit 111

Armstrong Air & Space Museum

Driving time:	2 minutes
Ages:	6 and up
Length of visit:	1–3 hours
Address:	500 South Apollo Drive Wapakoneta, OH 45895
Directions:	Take exit 111 (Bellefontaine Street/Wapakoneta) and go west 0.3 mile. Turn right on South Apollo Drive, which takes you to the Armstrong Air & Space Museum parking lot. Directions are signed from I-75.
Cost:	$7 adults $3 children (ages 6–12) Free for children under 6
Hours:	Tue–Sat 9:30 a.m.–5 p.m., Sundays and holidays noon–5 p.m. Closed Thanksgiving Day, Christmas Day, and New Year's Day.
Phone:	(800) 860-0142
Web site:	http://www.ohiohistory.org/places/armstron/
Description and comments:	Neil Armstrong was the first human to set foot on the moon and grew up in nearby Wapakoneta. The Armstrong Air & Space Museum is a tribute to him and a must-stop for space lovers.

NASA Mission Control and Neil Armstrong, July 20, 1969

"Eagle . . . you're go for a landing."
"Roger . . . picking up some dust . . . big shadow . . . contact light . . .
O.K., engine stopped. Tranquility Base here. The Eagle has landed."

This museum traces the history of flight: exhibits include airplane prototypes, hot-air balloons, and the evolution of aircraft and spacecraft. Apollo 11 artifacts, moon rock, and meteorite samples are on display. Be sure to watch the 25-minute movie about Americans in space. This museum is best for school-age children and older, as there are limited hands-on activities to keep the attention of toddlers and preschoolers. However, younger kids that really love outer space may also enjoy this museum. Our kids enjoyed learning about what is needed in order to become an astronaut (physical size, education, etc.).

Exit 104

Botkins Community Park

Driving time:	2 minutes
Ages:	2 and up
Length of visit:	1 hour
Address:	502 East State Street, Botkins, OH 45306
Directions:	Take exit 104 (Route 219/Botkins) and go west 0.3 mile. Turn right on the small road with the Community Park sign (just past the first gas station) to Botkins Community Park.
Cost:	Free
Hours:	Dawn–dusk
Web site:	http://www.botkinsohio.com/park.htm
Description and comments:	Take a break and relax at this nice outdoor community park. Sports enthusiasts can visit the volleyball, tennis, basketball, and soccer facilities. Kids will love the large outdoor playground structure, swings, and merry-go-round. Restrooms and seasonal concessions are also available.

Exit 92

McDonald's with an Outdoor Play Area

Driving time:	2 minutes
Directions:	Take exit 92 (OH-47/Versailles/Sidney) and go west 0.5 mile. McDonald's is on the left.

Exit 82

McDonald's with a Tented Outdoor Play Area
Miami Valley Centre Mall

McDonald's with a Tented Outdoor Play Area

Driving time:	2 minutes
Directions:	Take exit 82 (US 36/Piqua/Urbana) and go west 0.3 mile. Turn left at the Miami Valley Centre Mall parking lot.
Comments:	The play area is closed when it rains.

Miami Valley Centre Mall

Driving time:	2 minutes
Ages:	2 and up
Length of visit:	1–2 hours
Address:	987 East Ash Street, Piqua, OH 45356
Directions:	Take exit 82 (US 36/Piqua/Urbana) and go west 0.3 mile. Turn left on Scott Drive to Miami Valley Centre Mall.
Cost:	Free

Hours:	Mon–Sat 10 a.m.–9 p.m., Sun noon–6 p.m.
	Closed Easter, Thanksgiving Day, and Christmas Day.
Phone:	(937) 773-1225
Web site:	http://www.miamivalleycentremall.com/
Description and comments:	This mall has anchor stores including Sears, JCPenney, and Elder-Beerman. Families will enjoy the large arcade, movie theater, and limited food court. Toddlers will enjoy the small coin-operated ride area.

Ohio Mile Marker 80

Rest Area

This rest area has restrooms, telephones, vending machines, picnic tables, and space for kids to run.

Exit 74

McDonald's with an Outdoor Play Area

Driving time:	1 minute
Directions:	Take exit 74 (OH-41/Troy) and go east 0.1 mile to McDonald's.

Exit 68

McDonald's with an Indoor Play Area

Driving time:	1 minute
Directions:	Take exit 68 (OH-571/West Milton/Tipp City) and go east 0.2 mile. McDonald's is on the right.

Exit 63

McDonald's with an Indoor Play Area
Burger King with an Indoor Play Area

McDonald's with an Indoor Play Area

Driving time: 1 minute

Directions: Take exit 63 (Route 40/Vandalia/Donnelsville) and go west 0.1 mile. McDonald's is on the left.

Burger King with an Indoor Play Area

Driving time: 1 minute

Directions: Take exit 63 (Route 40/Vandalia/Donnelsville) and go west 0.3 mile. Burger King is on the left.

Kid Trivia

The Wright Brothers grew up in Dayton, Ohio. They went to school, ran their bicycle business, and built their famous *Wright Flyer* in Dayton. The plane was taken to Kitty Hawk, North Carolina, for the famous first flight in 1903.

Exit 58 or 54C

National Museum of the United States Air Force

Driving time: 12 minutes heading south
7 minutes heading north

Ages: 8 and up

Length of visit: 2–5 hours

Address: 1100 Spaatz Street
Wright Patterson Air Force Base, OH 45433

Directions heading south:	Take exit 58 (Needmore Road) and turn left to head east 6 miles on Needmore Road (Needmore Road becomes Harshman Road). Turn right on Springfield Pike and go 0.5 mile. The entrance to the museum is on the right. You can follow brown signs to the museum starting on Harshman Road.
Directions heading north:	Take exit 54C (OH-4 north) and go 3.5 miles. Take the OH-4 Harshman Road exit and turn right on Harshman Road. Go 1 mile and turn right on Springfield Pike. The museum is 0.5 mile ahead on the right. You can follow brown signs to the museum starting on OH-4.
Cost:	Free (donations are appreciated) Parking: Free IMAX admission: $6 adults $5.50 seniors (ages 60 and up) $4.50 children (ages 8–college) $3 children (ages 3–7) Free for children under 3
Hours:	9 a.m.–5 p.m. Closed New Year's Day, Thanksgiving Day, and Christmas Day.

The World War I fighter plane SPAD XIII
(Courtesy of the National Museum of the United States Air Force)

Phone:	(937) 255-3286
Web site:	http://www.wpafb.af.mil/museum
Description and comments:	As you pull into the parking lot of the National Museum of the United States Air Force, you realize you are at a special place. The beautifully manicured USAF Museum Memorial Park leads you to the main building. Inside is the Air Force's national museum and the largest and oldest aviation museum in the world, with approximately 17 acres of exhibits. This attraction features nearly 350 authentic aircraft and missiles, plus thousands of personal artifacts, documents, photographs and mementos of Air Force history from the early 1900s to the present. Highlights include the first permanent display of a B-2 stealth bomber, a collection of presidential aircraft, and plenty of rare aircraft.

This is a must-stop for any aircraft lover or anyone interested in the Air Force or world wars. The museum is a hands-off museum: toddlers and preschoolers may not enjoy this stop after the awe of seeing huge aircraft up close is over. The motion simulator rides are best suited for school-age kids and older. An indoor cafeteria is open year round, and an outdoor cafeteria is open seasonally on weekends.

Exit 57B

Boonshoft Museum of Discovery

Driving time:	6 minutes
Ages:	All
Length of visit:	2–4 hours
Address:	2600 DeWeese Parkway, Dayton, OH 45414

Directions: Take exit 57B (Wagoner Ford Road/Sieben-
thaler Avenue) and go west on Wagoner Ford
Road 0.2 mile. Turn right on North Dixie Drive,
immediately get into the left lane, turn left on
Siebenthaler Avenue, and go 0.4 mile. Turn left
on Ridge Avenue and go 1 mile. Turn right on
DeWeese Parkway. The museum is on the right.
You can follow the brown signs to the museum
from Siebenthaler Avenue.

Cost: $8.50 adults
$7 seniors (ages 62 and up)
$7 children (ages 2–12)
Free for children under 2

Parking: Free

This museum is a member of ASTC, ACM, AZA.

Hours: Mon–Fri 9 a.m.–5 p.m.,
Sat 11 a.m.–5 p.m., Sun noon–5 p.m.

Closed Easter, Thanksgiving Day, Christmas
Eve, Christmas Day, New Year's Eve, and New
Year's Day.

Touching starfish at the tidal pool at Boonshoft Museum of Discovery

Phone: (937) 275-7431

Web site: http://www.boonshoftmuseum.org/

Description and Boonshoft Museum of Discovery is a wonder-
comments: ful science museum for visitors of all ages. The
museum packs numerous activities into a rela-
tively small area. Everyone can enjoy playing at
the water table, climbing the tree house, viewing native Ohio animals at the zoo, and learning
about planets in the space area. Kids aged 6 and
under have a place of their own where they can
enjoy a water table, see miniature houses, and
dig for dinosaur bones without the pressures of
sharing with older children. You will also find
a similar area for kids aged 2 and under. Our
kids especially liked shopping in the grocery
store, taking care of ailing stuffed animals at the
animal hospital, recycling trash, and touching
starfish and sea anemones in the tidal pool touch
tank (open only 2 hours a day). Our whole family
enjoyed the space theater show *The Sky Tonight*
($1 extra for nonmembers), which showed us
how to find planets in the night sky for the date
on which we visited and even took us for a ride
through a virtual black hole.

Be sure to get a copy of the Things to Do Today
sheet at the front desk for a listing of shows and
activities for the day. If you get hungry, sit down
and have a snack at the vending-machine area
(there is no restaurant here). If you don't get
worn out at the museum, use the walking/biking
trail along DeWeese Parkway, directly across the
street from the museum.

Exit 44

Dayton Mall
Cox Arboretum MetroPark

Dayton Mall

Driving time:	3 minutes
Ages:	2 and up
Length of visit:	1–2 hours
Address:	2700 Miamisburg-Centerville Road Dayton, OH 45459
Directions:	Take exit 44 (Route 725/Miamisburg) and go east 0.4 mile. The Dayton Mall is on the right.
Cost:	Free
Hours:	Mon–Sat 10 a.m.–9 p.m., Sun noon–6 p.m.
Phone:	(937) 433-9834
Web site:	http://www.daytonmall.net/
Description and comments:	Stretch your legs at the Dayton Mall. This is a major mall, with anchor stores including Sears, Macy's, JCPenney, and Elder-Beerman. There is a food court, a merry-go-round (with a spinning teacup for older kids), small coin-operated rides, and an arcade.

Cox Arboretum MetroPark

Driving time:	5 minutes
Ages:	2 and up
Length of visit:	1–2 hours
Address:	6733 Springboro Pike, Dayton, OH 45449

Directions: Take exit 44 (Route 725/Miamisburg) and go east 0.4 mile. Turn left on Springboro Pike (OH-741) and go 1.3 miles. Cox Arboretum MetroPark is on the left.

Cost: Free

Hours: Park: 8 a.m.–dusk

Visitor center: Mon–Fri 8:30 a.m.–4:30 p.m., Weekends 1 p.m.–4 p.m.

Closed Christmas Day and New Year's Day.

Phone: (937) 434-9005

Web site: http://www.metroparks.org/
Click on Facilities & Parks.

Description and comments: Enjoy the beautifully manicured gardens and wonderful views of the Cox Arboretum MetroPark. There are 160 acres of trees and plants as well as water gardens, walking paths, and trails (paved and unpaved). Stop by the education building to see a nature movie. Kids love to look at the large koi and numerous turtles in the pond near the entrance. This is a great park for a picnic or a quick break.

Cincinnati Driving

If you are heading south, you're now getting close to the Cincinnati area. Try to avoid rush-hour traffic on I-75 through Cincinnati. We advise you not to drive through Cincinnati between 7 a.m. and 8:30 a.m. or between 4 p.m. and 6 p.m. on weekdays. If you must drive through the area during these times, we suggest you take I-275 west around Cincinnati. The other option is to call ARTIMIS (Advanced Regional Traffic Interactive Management & Information System) by dialing 511. After the prompts, dial 751 and then dial 752 to get information on traffic flow from mile marker 22 through Cincinnati. You can also check traffic conditions on I-275. Visit http://www.artimis.org/ for further details.

Ohio Mile Marker 28

Rest Area

This rest area has restrooms, vending machines, telephones, picnic tables, and space for kids to run.

Exit 22

McDonald's with an Outdoor Play Area

Driving time:	1 minute
Directions:	Take exit 22 (Tylersville Road/Hamilton) and go east 0.1 mile. McDonald's is on the right.

Exit 16

Dave & Buster's
Tri-County Mall
Cincinnati Mills Mall

Dave & Buster's

Driving time:	11 minutes
Ages:	3 and up
Length of visit:	1–2 hours
Address:	11775 Commons Drive, Springdale, OH 45246
Directions:	Take exit 16 (I-275 west) and head west 2 miles. Take I-275 exit 42A (OH-747 South) toward Springdale and Glendale and go 0.8 mile. Turn left on Kemper Road and go 0.7 mile. Turn left on Commons Road and go 0.5 mile. Dave & Buster's is on the left.

Cost:	Admission: Free
	Purchase a debit card to play games.
	Expect to pay $1–$3 per game.
Hours:	Sun–Wed 11:30 a.m.–midnight,
	Thu 11:30 a.m.–1 a.m.,
	Fri–Sat 11:30 a.m.–2 a.m.
Phone:	(513) 671-5501
Web site:	http://www.daveandbusters.com
Description and comments:	Stop and play arcade games at Dave & Buster's. You will also find many ride simulation games and activities like Skee-Ball. This is a good place during the day for families with kids; however, in the late evening patrons are mostly adults.

Tri-County Mall

Driving time:	4 minutes
Ages:	All
Length of visit:	1–2 hours
Address:	11700 Princeton Pike, Cincinnati, OH 45246
Directions:	Take exit 16 (I-275 west) and head west 2 miles. Take I-275 exit 42A (OH-747 south) toward Springdale and Glendale and go 0.4 mile. The Tri-County Mall is on the left.
Cost:	Free
Hours:	Mon–Sat 10 a.m.–9 p.m., Sun noon–6 p.m.
Phone:	(513) 346-4482
Web site:	http://www.tricountymall.com
Description and comments:	Visit over 170 stores anchored by Macy's, Dillard's, and Sears. For $1.50, toddlers will enjoy the train ride near the ample food court. The Kidzone play area is located between Dillard's

and Macy's, on the second floor. This play area is well equipped with riding and climbing toys for kids aged 5 and under.

Cincinnati Mills Mall

Driving time:	7 minutes
Ages:	All
Length of visit:	2 hours
Address:	600 Cincinnati Mills Drive Cincinnati, OH 45240
Directions:	Take exit 16 (I-275 west) and head west 5 miles. Take I-275 exit 39 (Winton Road) toward Fairfield and Forest Park. Keep right at the fork in the exit ramp toward South Gilmore Road and Fairfield. Turn right on South Gilmore Road and go 0.1 mile. Turn right on Cincinnati Mills Drive.
Cost:	Mall: Free Unlimited-ride passes (for rides only, arcade games are separate): $6 kids shorter than 36 inches $11 all others Lunar Golf: $6 adults $3 children (ages 5 and under) WonderPark: Single ride tickets $1–$2
Hours:	Mall: Mon–Sat 10 a.m.–9 p.m., Sun 11 a.m.–7 p.m. Outdoor World: Mon–Sat 9 a.m.–10 p.m., Sun 10 a.m.–7 p.m. WonderPark: Mon–Sat 10 a.m.–9 p.m., Sun 11 a.m.–7 p.m.
Phone:	Cincinnati Mills Mall: (513) 671-7467 Outdoor World: (513) 826-5200 WonderPark: (513) 671-0100
Web sites:	http://www.cincinnatimills.com/ http://www.basspro.com/ http://www.wonderparkusa.com/

Description and   Visit the largest mall in the Cincinnati area and
comments: our family's favorite mall on I-75. Cincinnati
                      Mills Mall was re-opened in August 2004 (it was
                      previously named Forest Fair Mall). It offers
                      numerous family-related activities. Located on
                      the first floor near entrance 2, WonderPark is an
                      indoor entertainment park for families with chil-
                      dren aged 2–12. Rides include a centipede train,
                      small bumper cars, a soft tree-house play area,
                      and a roller coaster. Just outside WonderPark is
                      A Place to Grow. Here kids aged 5 and under can
                      climb on soft, giant toy bugs and play games or
                      hear stories on the interactive touchscreens. Also
                      nearby is Lunar Golf, where you can play glow-
                      in-the-dark miniature golf. On the second floor,
                      kids aged 5–12 will enjoy PBS Kids Backyard,
                      where they can climb and slide on a play struc-
                      ture, look through a telescope, play memory
                      games, and watch PBS Kids shows in their own
                      miniature theater. Be sure to take a walk through
                      Johnny's Toys on the second floor, which is one
                      of the best toy stores we've visited. Kids can shop
                      for their favorite toy or play with the Thomas the
                      Tank Engine & Friends or Jay Jay the Jet Plane
                      set. Our kids really enjoyed the great selection of
                      huge lifelike stuffed animals. Dads (or any hunter
                      or angler in the family) will want to visit Bass Pro
                      Shops Outdoor World. Be sure to look at the
                      aquarium that holds huge native Ohio fish. An
                      adequate food court is located on the first floor.

Buckeyes

The buckeye tree is the state tree of Ohio. The word *buckeye* derives from
buck, a male white-tailed deer; the large brown seeds from the buckeye
tree resemble the eyes of a buck. Indians would often fish by putting
toxic, ground-up buckeyes in local waters. The stunned fish would float
to the surface.

Exit 14

Highfield Discovery Garden

Driving time:	4 minutes
Ages:	All
Length of visit:	2 hours
Address:	10405 Springfield Pike, Cincinnati, OH 45215
Directions:	Take exit 14 (Glendale-Milford Road) and head west toward Woodlawn for 1.6 miles. Glendale-Milford Road ends at Glenwood Gardens. Park in the Glenwood Gardens parking lot.
Cost:	Glenwood Gardens parking: $2 per vehicle
	Highfield Discovery Garden admission: $4 adults $3 children (ages 2–12) Free for children under 2
Hours:	November–March, Wed–Sat 10 a.m.–5 p.m., Sun noon–5 p.m.
	April–September, Tue–Sat 10 a.m.–6 p.m., Sun noon–6 p.m.
	October, Tue–Sat 10 a.m.–5 p.m., Sun noon–5 p.m.
Phone:	(513) 771–8733
Web site:	http://www.discoverygarden.org
Description and comments:	Highfield Discovery Garden is located within Glenwood Gardens. Both provide a great break from Cincinnati-area traffic. You can pay the $2 parking fee and visit Glenwood Gardens, where you can enjoy walking trails that include a 1-mile, fully accessible paved loop and a 1.5-mile gravel trail that passes a small wetland. To enter Highfield Discovery Garden, you must pay an additional entrance fee. Within the Highfield Discovery Garden you will find several themed outdoor gardens, including designs to attract butterflies and caterpillars. The Discovery Tree is

a large outdoor artificial tree full of crawling tubes, climbing structures, and pretend animals that toddlers and preschoolers will like. Kids can also have a make-believe tea party in a playhouse, learn about nature in the activity house, and view the outdoor model trains.

Exit 6

Cincinnati Zoo & Botanical Garden

Driving time:	5 minutes
Ages:	All
Length of visit:	2–5 hours
Address:	3400 Vine Street, Cincinnati, OH 45220
Directions:	Take exit 6 (Mitchell Avenue) and go east 0.4 mile. Turn right on Vine Street and follow signs to zoo parking. You can follow signs to the zoo from I-75.
Cost:	$12.95 adults $10.95 seniors (ages 62 and up) $7.95 children (ages 2–12) Free for children under 2

Cincinnati Zoo Makes History!

The Sumatran rhinoceros is considered one of the most endangered mammals on earth. Today fewer than 300 survive in the wild and only eight in captivity. In 2001 Emi, the zoo's female Sumatran rhinoceros, gave birth to a healthy calf named Andalas. This was the first time in 112 years that a Sumatran rhinoceros successfully reproduced in captivity. Then, the Cincinnati Zoo & Botanical Garden proudly announced on July 30, 2004, that Emi had given birth once again. She became the first Sumatran rhino in history to produce two calves in captivity. These two calves serve as a lifeline for a species clinging to survival.

An Asian elephant taking a bath at the Vanishing Giants exhibit
(Photo courtesy of David Jenike, Cincinnati Zoo & Botanical Garden)

Parking: $6.50

All-day ride pass for the train, shuttle, and carousel: $5.00

This zoo is a member of AZA.

Hours: 9 a.m.–5 p.m.

Operating hours can be variable, especially around the holidays. See the zoo Web site or call for current hours.

Closed Thanksgiving Day and Christmas Day.

Phone: (800) 944-4776

Web site: http://www.cincinnatizoo.org

Description and comments: A leading family travel guide rated the Cincinnati Zoo & Botanical Garden as one of the top zoos in the country. This second oldest zoo in the United States includes the Vanishing Giants exhibit featuring elephants, giraffes, and okapis, Lords of the Arctic where you can view polar bears both above and under water, Reptile House, Gorilla World, Manatee Springs (which are indoors), Children's Zoo, and many other exhibits. Toddlers and preschoolers will love the Children's Zoo, where they can view farm animals, feed the miniature goats (a favorite!), and even crawl inside a turtle shell or climb on a pretend spider web. A miniature train, carousel, and an outdoor playground round out the great activities for children. Nature lovers will also enjoy viewing over 3,000 species of plants. In fact, the Cincinnati Zoo & Botanical Garden is one of only two accredited botanical gardens in Ohio. This is a wonderful zoo, and the entire family should enjoy this trip. Our kids especially enjoyed the train ride around the zoo.

Exit 2A or 1G

Cincinnati Museum Center at Union Terminal

Driving time:	4 minutes
Ages:	All
Length of visit:	2–5 hours
Address:	1301 Western Avenue, Cincinnati, OH 45203
Directions heading south:	Take exit 2A (Western Avenue/Liberty Street) and go 0.5 mile. Turn right on Ezzard Charles Drive. Parking is on either side of Ezzard Charles Drive. You can follow signs to the Cincinnati Museum Center from I-75.
Directions heading north:	Take exit 1G (US 50 west), immediately north of the Brent Spence Bridge over the Ohio River. Stay in the left lane on US 50 and take the Gest Street exit immediately on the left. Turn right on Gest Street and go 0.5 mile. Turn right on Freeman Avenue and go 0.3 mile. Turn left on Ezzard Charles Drive to the Museum Center. Parking is on either side of Ezzard Charles Drive. You can follow signs to the Cincinnati Museum Center from I-75.

Cost:	Admission to each museum: $7.25 adults $6.25 seniors (ages 60 and up) $5.25 children (ages 3–12) $4.25 children ages 1 and 2 (an all-museum pass plus admission to an Omnimax movie) Free for children under 1
	Combination tickets to all three museums: $13.25 adults $9.25 children (ages 3–12)
	Parking: $4.50
	The Cincinnati Museum Center is a member of ASTC. Cinergy Children's Museum is a member of ACM.
Hours:	Mon–Sat 10 a.m.–5 p.m., Sun 11 a.m.–6 p.m.
	Closed Thanksgiving Day and Christmas Day.
Phone:	(800) 733-2077
Web site:	http://www.cincymuseum.org/
Description and comments:	This is one of our favorite stops along I-75 and there is plenty to enjoy for the entire family. Cincinnati Museum Center includes Cincinnati History Museum, Cinergy Children's Museum, and Museum of Natural History & Science. The museum center complex also hosts temporary exhibits as well as holiday theme exhibits (Boofest around Halloween and Holiday Junction between Thanksgiving and New Year's Day). Food (burgers, pizza, ice cream, etc.) is available in the main lobby. There is also an Omnimax movie theater.
	Cincinnati History Museum shows the history of Cincinnati, including a replica of the Cincinnati river front in the middle 1800s with many working small-scale trains. Any small-scale train lover or Cincinnati history buff will truly enjoy this area. Youngsters can play with the Thomas the Tank Engine & Friends train table. If there is anyone in your group who appreciates World War II exhibits, the Cincinnati Goes to War exhibit is a must-see.

The recreated Kentucky limestone cave at the
Museum of Natural History & Science at the
Cincinnati Museum Center (Photo courtesy of the
Cincinnati Museum Center at Union Terminal)

Cinergy Children's Museum has many hands-on exhibits designed for children aged 9 and under. These include a water play area, a large ball area, the Woods indoor tree house, a construction site, and a large indoor play area only for children under age 4. This is an excellent children's museum with plenty to do for kids of all ages.

Museum of Natural History & Science includes a walk through a glacier, a garbage and recycling display, fossil displays, and a hands-on discovery area. Younger kids really enjoy the sandbox play area, complete with a train table and other items for kids aged 5 and under. Our kids also like looking at and touching fossils, bones, and shells in the Trading Post. Be sure to check out the human body area, where kids can floss giant teeth, play with a "digestion" pinball machine (with bodily noises), and learn more about the human body. Lastly, everyone seems to enjoy walking through the artificial cave, complete with live bats! Our experience is that the Museum of Natural History & Science is a great place to go if the Children's Museum gets too crowded or the kids (or parents) need to wind down a little.

Exit 1C

Cincinnati Fire Museum

Driving time:	4 minutes
Ages:	4 and up
Length of visit:	1 hour
Address:	315 West Court Street, Cincinnati, OH 45202
Directions:	Take exit 1C (Downtown/5th Street) in Ohio (be sure to take 5th Street in Ohio, not 5th Street in Kentucky). Go 0.2 mile on 5th Street and turn left on Elm Street (just past the Cincinnati Convention Center). Go 0.5 mile on Elm Street, turn left on West Court Street and go 0.3 mile. The Cincinnati Fire Museum is on the left. Metered parking is available on the street in front of the museum.
Cost:	$6 adults $5 seniors (ages 54 and up) $4 children (ages 2–12) Free to children under 2
Hours:	Tue–Fri 10 a.m.–4 p.m., Weekends noon–4 p.m. Closed holidays.
Phone:	(513) 621–5553
Web site:	http://www.cincyfiremuseum.com/
Description and comments:	The Cincinnati Fire Museum chronicles Cincinnati's firefighting history. Preschoolers will enjoy hands-on exhibits, including a fire truck on which they can operate the lights, a firefighter's pole they can slide down, and a fire safety house. Older children and adults will like viewing the restored antique firefighting equipment, memorabilia, and photographs.

Exit 1A
Sawyer Point Park
The Cincinnati Reds Hall of Fame and Museum
National Underground Railroad Freedom Center

Sawyer Point Park

Driving time:	8 minutes
Ages:	2 and up
Length of visit:	1 hour
Address:	705 East Pete Rose Way, Cincinnati, OH 45202
Directions:	Take exit 1A (Downtown/2nd Street) and get in the right lane to 2nd Street. Go east 0.6 mile on 2nd Street. Follow signs to Pete Rose Way. Turn left on Pete Rose Way and go 0.5 mile. Turn right at Eggleston Avenue into Bicentennial Commons at Sawyer Point.
Cost:	Free
	Parking: $2 typical
	$5 on days of events such as Reds home games
Hours:	Dawn–dusk
Phone:	(513) 352-6180
Web site:	http://www.sawyerpoint.com/
Description and comments:	Walk along the Ohio River, or let the kids play on the large outdoor playground to your left as you enter the main gate. Our family enjoys viewing markers of the various historical flood stages of the Ohio River (kids think it is cool that you can stand where there was a river at one time). We also enjoy walking down the steps to the banks of the Ohio River and watching the boats and barges go by. This area is within walking distance of Great American Ballpark, home of the Cincinnati Reds, and the Cincinnati Reds Hall of Fame and Museum.

The Cincinnati Reds Hall of Fame and Museum

Driving time:	3 minutes
Ages:	3 and up
Length of visit:	2 hours
Address:	100 Main Street, Cincinnati, OH 45202
Directions heading south:	Take exit 1A (Downtown/2nd Street) and stay in the left lane. Turn left on Elm Street and go 0.1 mile. Turn left on 3rd Street and go 0.2 mile. Stay in the left lane. Turn left on Central Avenue and go 0.2 mile. Turn left on Pete Rose Way and go straight to Central Riverfront garage parking. After parking, walk 1 block east on 2nd Street to the museum, located directly west of Great American Ballpark, home of the Cincinnati Reds.
Directions heading north:	Take exit 1A (Downtown/2nd Street) and stay in the right lane. Go 0.3 mile on 2nd Street. Turn right on Elm Street and go 0.2 mile. Turn right on Mehring Way and go 0.2 mile. Turn right on Central Avenue and go 0.2 mile. Turn right on Pete Rose Way and go straight to Central Riverfront garage. After parking, walk 1 block east on 2nd Street to the museum, located directly west of Great American Ballpark, home of the Cincinnati Reds.
Cost:	$8 adults $6 seniors (ages 55 and up) $5 children (ages 3–12) Free for children under 3 Parking: $4 at Central Riverfront garage
Hours:	Off-season: Tue–Sat 10 a.m.–5 p.m. In-season: Mon–Sat 10 a.m.–5 p.m., Cincinnati Reds home game days: Open to same-day ticket holders only Closed Thanksgiving Day and Christmas Day.
Phone:	(513) 765–7000

Web site: http://www.cincinnatireds.com/
                        Click on Ballpark, Great American Ballpark, and
                        Hall of Fame and Museum.

Description and   Visit one of the top baseball museums in the
comments: country, dedicated to the Cincinnati Reds. Base-
                        ball fans of any age will enjoy the Cincinnati
                        Reds Hall of Fame and Museum, which opened
                        in 2004. Adults will like the photographs, memo-
                        rabilia, and displays, while kids will enjoy the
                        hands-on exhibits. At the Fence is where kids
                        (and grown-up kids) can catch a baseball to pre-
                        vent a homerun over the fence. Kids can learn
                        how to throw a curveball, learn how to bat, or
                        visit the Kid's Clubhouse, where they can put on
                        uniforms and crawl in a soft play area. Be sure to
                        check out You Make the Call, where you get to be
                        the play-by-play announcer of some memorable
                        Reds events over the microphone. Then you get
                        to hear how the professionals made the call. Our
                        favorite activity was the pitching area, where you
                        get to throw a baseball from the pitcher's mound
                        to the batter's strike zone. Hopefully you have a
                        more accurate and faster pitch than we do!

National Underground Railroad Freedom Center

Driving time: 3 minutes

Ages: 6 and up

Length of visit: 2–4 hours

Address: 50 East Freedom Way, Cincinnati, OH 45202

Directions   Take exit 1A (Downtown/2nd Street) and stay in
heading south: the left lane. Turn left on Elm Street and go 0.1
                        mile. Turn left on 3rd Street and go 0.2 mile. Turn
                        left on Central Avenue and go 0.2 mile. Turn left
                        on Pete Rose Way and go straight to Central Riv-
                        erfront garage parking. Take the garage elevator
                        to the street level to the National Underground
                        Railroad Freedom Center.

Directions heading north:	Take exit 1A (Downtown/2nd Street) and stay in the right lane. Go 0.3 mile on 2nd Street. Turn right on Elm Street and go 0.2 mile. Turn right on Mehring Way and go 0.2 mile. Turn right on Central Avenue and go 0.2 mile. Turn right on Pete Rose Way and go straight to Central Riverfront garage. Take the garage elevator to street level to the National Underground Railroad Freedom Center.
Cost:	$12 adults $10 students with ID, seniors (ages 60 and up) $8 children (ages 6–12) Free for children under 6 Parking: $4 at Central Riverfront garage
Hours:	Tue–Sun 11 a.m.–5 p.m. Closed Thanksgiving Day and Christmas Day. Due to parking conflicts, the museum may be closed at other times. Call before you plan your trip.
Phone:	(877) 648–4838
Web site:	http://www.freedomcenter.org/
Description and comments:	Open since August 2004, the National Underground Railroad Freedom Center describes Cincinnati's role in the Underground Railroad. In the 1800s, the city served as a major hub of activity on the Underground Railroad. Thousands of slaves crossed the Ohio River to Cincinnati to seek refuge. See the 15-minute film *Brothers of the Borderland* when you arrive. This movie, which includes Oprah Winfrey, commemorates local abolitionist heroes in an "environmental theater" with natural sounds, trees, and mist to replicate a nighttime setting. The film sets the tone of the museum. Other exhibits feature artifacts, timelines, and fascinating stories of hundreds of railroad participants. Visitors can even walk inside an actual slave pen. This museum is a must-see for adults. There may not be enough hands-on activities to keep the attention of those under age 6. Food is available.

Kentucky

Top Kentucky Family Stops

Newport Aquarium
Florence Aquatic Center
Kentucky Horse Park
Explorium of Lexington
Levi Jackson Wilderness Road State Park

Kentucky Quick View

Attraction	Kentucky Exit Number
Zoo or Aquarium	192
Park	186, 181, 180, 175, 171, 95, 38
Museum	113, 29
Mall	192, 180A/180
Family Entertainment Center	191, 181, 180A/180, 178, 110, 11
Rest Area Mile Marker	177, 127, 83, 2 (northbound only)
Fast Food with an Indoor Play Area	181, 180, 159, 108, 76, 62, 38, 25, 11
Fast Food with an Outdoor Play Area	186, 180, 175, 159, 38, 29
Other Attraction	185, 181, 120, 87, 77

Kentucky Emergency Information

Emergency Phone:	911
Kentucky State Police Hotline:	(800) 222–5555 (or 511 in KY)
Exits with Police Sign:	166, 159, 87, 41
Exits with Hospital Sign:	185, 182, 156, 126, 125, 120, 108, 104, 87, 76, 62, 41, 38, 25

Exit 192
Newport on the Levee
Newport Aquarium

Newport on the Levee

Driving time: 8 minutes

Ages: 2 and up

Length of visit: 1–3 hours

Address: One Levee Way, Newport, KY 41071

Directions: Take exit 192 (5th Street) in Kentucky (not 5th Street in Ohio), and head east on 5th Street (Route 8). Follow Route 8 for 2.5 miles to the Levee and Aquarium parking garage. There are several other parking lots in the area. You can follow the shark signs to the Levee and Aquarium parking garage from I-75.

Cost: Admission: Free

Parking: $3–$5 in the Levee parking garage

Hours: September–May, Mon–Thu 11 a.m.–9 p.m., Fri–Sat 11 a.m.–10 p.m., Sun noon–6 p.m.

June–August, Mon–Thu 10 a.m.–9 p.m., Fri–Sat 10 a.m.–10 p.m., Sun noon–6 p.m.

Closed Easter, Thanksgiving Day, and Christmas Day.

Phone: (866) 538-3359

Web site: http://www.newportonthelevee.com/

Description and comments: A major family travel guide rated Newport on the Levee the number one mall or shopping attraction in the United States for families. Newport on the Levee is a 10-acre "town square" mall complex that includes 10 restaurants, 21 shopping venues, a live cabaret, a comedy club, a jazz and blues club, a 20-screen stadium-style seating theater, live music, street performers, artists, magicians, a Gameworks arcade complex, the Newport Aquarium (see below), and a great view of the Ohio River and downtown Cincinnati, Ohio. On a nice day, be sure to walk across the Ohio River on the pedestrian-only purple bridge. Once across the bridge on the Ohio side, walk along the river 3 blocks east to get to a large outdoor playground.

KY 511

Dial 511 to get travel information and interstate road conditions anywhere in Kentucky. This is a voice-recognition system, and you can get operator help if you need it.

You can also visit http://www.511.ky.gov/ on the Web before you travel to check conditions on I-75 through Kentucky.

Newport Aquarium

Driving time:	8 minutes
Ages:	All
Length of visit:	2 hours
Address:	One Levee Way, Newport, KY 41071
Directions:	Take exit 192 (5th Street) in Kentucky (not 5th Street in Ohio), and head east on 5th Street (Route 8). Follow Route 8 for 2.5 miles to the Levee and Aquarium parking garage. There are several other parking lots in the area. You can follow the shark signs to the Levee and Aquarium parking garage from I-75.
Cost:	$17.95 adults $15.95 seniors (ages 65 and up) $10.95 children (ages 3–12) Free for children under 3

View from Surrounded by Sharks at the Newport Aquarium
(Photo courtesy of the Newport Aquarium)

Lorikeet nectar: $1

Parking: $3–$5 in the Levee parking garage

This aquarium is a member of AZA.

Hours: 10 a.m.–6 p.m.

Extended hours available during the summer and during promotional times. Call or see the Web site for current hours.

Phone: (859) 261-7444

Web site: http://www.newportaquarium.com/

Description and comments: Voted the number one aquarium in the Midwest by a leading family travel guide, the Newport Aquarium is a great family stop. This aquarium features nearly 600 species of animals, including tropical sharks, Antarctic penguins, American alligators, and fish from all over the world. There are 66 exhibits totaling one million gallons of fresh and salt water. Kids really enjoy the touch tank, where they can feel sea stars, hermit crabs, spider crabs, and horseshoe crabs. The other big attraction for kids young and old is the shark tunnel, where you walk through a long acrylic tunnel surrounded by sharks (the sand tiger sharks are very impressive), stingrays, and tropical fish. Adults seem more mesmerized by the wonderful jellyfish exhibits and by watching the penguins. The Hidden Treasures of the Rainforest Islands exhibit opened in 2004. Animals of Indonesia are displayed here, including lories and lorikeets, Burmese pythons, and Asian river otters. Both kids and adults enjoy feeding nectar to the lories and lorikeets.

Food is available in the aquarium or at nearby Newport on the Levee. Strollers can be used when the aquarium is not too crowded, but during times of peak attendance you may be required to use a backpack, obtained free of charge from the aquarium.

Kentucky Trivia

· Kentucky became the 15th state in 1792.

· The American Civil War presidents Abraham Lincoln (United States) and Jefferson Davis (Confederate States) were born in Kentucky, about 100 miles apart.

Exit 191

Jillian's

Driving time:	2 minutes
Ages:	3 and up
Length of visit:	1 hour
Address:	1200 Jillian's Way, Covington, KY 41011
Directions heading south:	Take exit 191 (12th Street/Pike Street/Covington) and go through the first light on the exit ramp. Turn left on 12th Street and go 0.1 mile. Turn left on Jillian's Way. Turn right into Jillian's parking lot for valet parking or turn left at Jillian's and park under the highway overpass for free parking.

Directions heading north:	Take exit 191 (12th Street/Pike Street/Covington) straight to Jillian's Way. Turn right into Jillian's parking lot for valet parking or turn left at Jillian's and park under the highway overpass for free parking.
Cost:	Admission: Free Purchase a debit card to play games. Expect to pay $1–$3 per game.
Hours:	Sun–Thu 11:30 a.m.–midnight, Fri–Sat 11:30 a.m.–2:30 a.m.
Phone:	(859) 491–5388
Web site:	http://www.jilliansbilliards.com/
Description and comments:	Jillian's is a complex with a huge array of arcade games, a sports bar (with food available), a bowling alley, and two restaurants. Kids aged 3 and up will enjoy playing arcade bowling, Skee-Ball, and many other interactive games. This is a good place for kids to play in the daytime; however, in the late evening patrons are mostly adults.

Exit 186

McDonald's with an Outdoor Play Area
Crescent Springs Community Park

McDonald's with an Outdoor Play Area

Driving time:	2 minutes
Directions:	Take exit 186 (KY-371/Buttermilk Pike) and go west 0.1 mile. Turn left on Hazelwood Road. McDonald's is on the left.

Crescent Springs Community Park

Driving time:	4 minutes
Ages:	1–12
Length of visit:	1 hour
Address:	800 Buttermilk Pike, Fort Mitchell, KY 41017
Directions:	Take exit 186 (KY-371/Buttermilk Pike) and head west 1 mile. Crescent Springs Community Park is on the right.
Cost:	Free
Hours:	8 a.m.–9 p.m.
Web site:	http://www.crescent-springs.ky.us/Recreation.htm
Description and comments:	This outdoor community park was designed for children ages 1–12. Enjoy the large, mulch-based playground with two play structure areas (one for younger kids and one for older), an unpaved hiking trail through the woods, horseshoe pits, basketball courts, and a soccer field. A covered picnic area, water fountains, and restrooms are available.

Exit 185

Totter's Otterville at Johnny's Toys

Driving time:	8 minutes
Ages:	Totter's Otterville: 10 and younger Johnny's Toys: All
Length of visit:	1–4 hours
Address:	4314 Boron Drive, Covington, KY 41015

Building at Totter's Otterville

Directions: Take exit 185 (I-275 east), and head east 3.5
                     miles. Take I-275 exit 80 (KY-17). Turn left off
                     the exit ramp and head north on KY-17 1.5 miles.
                     Turn right on Howard Litlzer Boulevard and go
                     0.5 mile. Johnny's Toys is on the right. Totter's
                     Otterville is inside Johnny's Toys.

Cost: Totter's Otterville:
                     Mon–Fri
                     $5.95 children (ages 10 and younger)
                     Free for adults

                     Weekends (Fri after 3 p.m., Sat, Sun, holidays)
                     $6.95 children (ages 10 and younger)
                     Free for adults

                     Johnny's Toys: Free

Hours: Totter's Otterville:
                     Mon–Sat 10 a.m.–8 p.m.,
                     Sun 11 a.m.–5 p.m.

                     Johnny's Toys:
                     Mon–Sat 10 a.m.–9 p.m.,
                     Sun 11 a.m.–6 p.m.

                     See Web site for holiday hours.

Phone:	Johnny's Toys: (859) 261-6962 Totter's Otterville: (859) 491-1441
Web site:	http://www.johnnystoys.com/
Description and comments:	Johnny's Toys is a large toy store with an emphasis on trains. Kids can play with the train tables set up near the front of the store or explore the hands-on model train exhibit. Inside Johnny's Toys is Totter's Otterville. After paying the Otterville entrance fee, kids can enjoy hands-on areas including a Thomas the Tank Engine & Friends train area, a miniature toy section with toy animals and dollhouses, a water play area (bring a change of clothes if your kids are attracted to water like our kids are), a ball pit and climbing zone, a pretend store, a dress-up boutique, and a special play place for kids younger than 18 months. If you are lucky, you may catch a "tea party," complete with free juice and cookies, or a puppet show. In the seasonal outdoor area, kids can have fun in an outdoor play structure, dig for dinosaur bones, run through a maze, do some pretend fishing, and even ride a miniature trolley. You can get subs, pizza, hot dogs, or chicken nuggets at the Otterville café. This is a great place for kids to explore and to burn some energy, and it is a family favorite of ours. Otterville uses a wristband system to help ensure that kids leave with the group they entered with.

Kid Trivia

Florence Y'all: Check out the water tower on the west side of I-75 near mile marker 181. The tower was used to advertise the nearby Florence Mall. But at the time (1974), the sign violated Kentucky highway regulations. The mayor of Florence suggested replacing "Mall" with "Y'all." The tower soon became an icon for the city of Florence.

Exit 181

World of Sports
Florence/Boone County Skate Park
Florence Aquatic Center
Sports of All Sorts
Burger King with an Indoor Play Area
Stringtown Park

World of Sports

Driving time:	2 minutes
Ages:	3 and up
Length of visit:	1 hour
Address:	7400 Woodspoint Drive, Florence, KY 41042
Directions:	Take exit 181 (KY-18/Florence/Burlington) and go west 0.1 mile. Turn right on Woodspoint Drive and go 0.2 mile. World of Sports is on the left.
Cost:	Miniature golf: $5 Free for children under 3
Hours:	8 a.m.–11 p.m.
Phone:	(859) 371–8255
Web site:	http://www.landrumgolf.com/
Description and comments:	Families can play on the lighted outdoor 18-hole miniature golf course. You'll find a snack bar and a small arcade inside. For the more serious golfer in your family, try the driving range or 18-hole golf course.

Florence/Boone County Skate Park

Driving time:	2 minutes
Ages:	6 and up

Length of visit:	1–2 hours
Address:	8100 Ewing Boulevard, Florence, KY 41042
Directions:	Take exit 181 (KY-18/Florence/Burlington) and go east 0.2 mile. Turn right on Ewing Boulevard. The Florence/Boone County Skate Park is immediately on the left. Free parking is available.
Cost:	Free
Hours:	Dawn–dusk
Web site:	http://www.cityofflorenceky.com/pr_skate_park.htm
Description and comments:	This outdoor, 20,000-square-foot park was designed for in-line skates and skateboards and is popular with the local skaters. It includes beginner, intermediate, and advanced areas. Be sure to bring proper safety equipment and your skates.

Florence Aquatic Center

Driving time:	2 minutes
Ages:	All
Length of visit:	2–4 hours
Address:	8100 Ewing Boulevard, Florence, KY 41042
Directions:	Take exit 181 (KY-18/Florence/Burlington) and go east 0.2 mile. Turn right on Ewing Boulevard. The aquatic center is on the left. Free parking is available.
Cost:	$8 adults $5 seniors (ages 65 and up) $5 children (ages 3–15) Free for children under 3
Hours:	Memorial Day weekend–mid-August Sun–Thu 11 a.m.–7 p.m., Fri–Sat 11 a.m.–8 p.m. Late August–Labor Day, Sat 11 a.m.–8 p.m., Sun 11 a.m.–7 p.m.

The octopus slide at the Florence Aquatic Center

Phone:	(859) 647–5439
Web site:	http://www.cityofflorenceky.com/pr_aquatic _center.htm
Description and comments:	The whole family should enjoy this aquatic center, which opened in 2003. Older kids and adults will enjoy the lazy river, competition pool (with diving boards), and two large water slides. Youngsters will love the huge zero-depth-entry shallow area and the two "spray grounds." One of the spray areas is just right for little ones under 3 years old. The center also has sunbathing areas, shelters, restrooms, and a concessions area.

Sports of All Sorts

Driving time:	3 minutes
Ages:	2 and up
Length of visit:	2 hours
Address:	25 Cavalier Boulevard, Florence, KY 41042

Directions:	Take exit 181 (KY-18/Florence/Burlington) and head east 1.4 miles. Sports of All Sorts is on the left.
Cost:	Admission: Free
	Soft play area: $2.95 Go-kart rides: $5 Bumper boat rides: $5
	Miniature golf: $5 adults $4 children (ages 3–12) Free for children under 3
Hours:	Sun–Thu 10 a.m.–10 p.m., Fri–Sat 10 a.m.–11 p.m.
Phone:	(859) 371-5511
Web site:	http://www.sportsofallsortsky.com/
Description and comments:	Need a good stop for a rainy day? Stop at this indoor and outdoor recreational complex for some fun. Inside, you can enjoy an arcade, pool tables, batting cages (softball and baseball), a basketball court, a soccer field, and a large soft play area. Seasonal outdoor activities include go-karts, bumper boats, and miniature golf. Food (pizza, etc.) is available near the soft play area. Note that there are two Sports of All Sorts locations. The same company runs them both, but each is unique. The other one is located at KY exit 178.

Burger King with an Indoor Play Area

Driving time:	6 minutes
Directions:	Take exit 181 (KY-18/Florence/Burlington) and head west 3 miles. Burger King is on the left.

Stringtown Park

Driving time:	2 minutes
Ages:	2 and up

Length of visit:	1 hour
Directions:	Take exit 181 (KY-18/Florence/Burlington) and go east 0.8 mile. Stringtown Park is on the left.
Cost:	Free
Hours:	Dawn–dusk
Web site:	http://www.cityofflorenceky.com/ Click on Parks and Recreation.
Description and comments:	This park, which opened in 2005, is a great outdoor park in the city of Florence. It has a basketball court and a nice playground. The playground, which has a very soft solid rubber base, includes slides, bridges, climbing areas, and swings. The restroom consists of a well-maintained portable toilet with hand sanitizers (no running water). There are no water fountains here. This is a great park for a quick break.

Exit 180A or 180
McDonald's with an Outdoor Play Area
Florence Mall
Burger King with an Indoor Play Area
Chuck E. Cheese
South Fork Park
Ockerman Park

McDonald's with an Outdoor Play Area

Driving time:	3 minutes
Directions:	Take exit 180 (US 42/US 127/Florence/Union) and go east 0.2 mile. Turn left on Dream Street. McDonald's is 0.3 mile ahead on the left.

Florence Mall

Driving time:	4 minutes
Ages:	All
Length of visit:	1 hour
Address:	2028 Florence Mall, Florence, KY 41042
Directions heading south:	Take exit 180A (Mall Road). Turn right off the exit and go 0.2 mile. Florence Mall is on the right.
Directions heading north:	Take exit 180 (US 42/US 127/Florence/Union). Turn left on US 42 and go 0.5 mile. Turn right on Mall Road and go 0.5 mile. Florence Mall is on the right.
Cost:	Free
Hours:	Mon–Sat 10 a.m.–9 p.m., Sun noon–6 p.m.
Phone:	(859) 371-1231
Web site:	http://www.florencemall.com/
Description and comments:	Stretch your legs and have a bite to eat at the Florence Mall. The food court includes Cincinnati-style chili, pizza, McDonald's, Chick-Fil-A, Chinese food, and several other dining spots. Our kids enjoy playing on the indoor soft wooly-mammoth play area (for kids 42 inches or shorter) on the first floor, near Macy's Home Store. Other anchor stores include JCPenney, Sears, and Macy's.

Need a Kid's Haircut?

Stop at the Kid's Corral in the small shopping center just behind Burger King. This is the place for good, fast, and reasonably priced cuts, with a fenced area for the kids to play in while you wait. Open Tuesday–Friday 10 a.m.–6:30 p.m., Saturday 9 a.m.–2:30 p.m.

Burger King with an Indoor Play Area

Driving time:	4 minutes
Directions:	Take exit 180 (US 42/US 127/Florence/Union) and go west 0.9 mile. Burger King is on the left.

Chuck E. Cheese

Driving time:	4 minutes
Ages:	2–12
Length of visit:	1–2 hours
Address:	7635 Mall Road, Florence, KY 41042
Directions heading south:	Take exit 180A (Mall Road). Turn right off the exit and go 0.4 mile. Chuck E. Cheese is on the left.
Directions heading north:	Take exit 180 (US 42/US 127/Florence/Union). Turn left on US 42 and go 0.5 mile. Turn right on Mall Road and go 0.7 mile. Chuck E. Cheese is on the left.
Cost:	Admission: Free
	Arcade tokens: $0.25 (all games one token)
Hours:	Sun–Thu 10 a.m.–9 p.m., Fri–Sat 10 a.m.–10 p.m.
Phone:	(859) 525-8835
Web site:	http://www.chuckecheese.com/
Description and comments:	Kids can play child-appropriate arcade games, crawl around in a climbing play area, or watch Chuck E. Cheese and his band play music. There's even a toddler zone with special games for the smallest players. If you get hungry, you can purchase pizza, sandwiches, and salads. This Chuck E. Cheese has a Kid Check program, in which a staff member stamps your group's hands

for identification. To make sure kids leave with the group they came with, a staff member checks their hand stamps as they exit. We like going to Chuck E. Cheese for driving stops as they are generally clean, safe, and give the kids a fun place to blow off steam while their parents relax.

Looking for a Hotel?

Our favorite hotel near Florence, Kentucky, is the Wildwood Inn, about 1 mile east of KY exit 180. For about $100, we get a poolside room with two double beds, and a continental breakfast. The real attraction here is the tropical dome, complete with a heated pool, a children's pool, a Jacuzzi, an arcade room, pool tables, and lots of palm trees to make you feel you are in a tropical jungle. You can get one of the themed suites (cave, speedway, oriental, etc.) in the outbuildings, which are spectacular, but you then need to walk to the tropical dome for a swim. AAA does not rate this hotel. Call (859) 371–6300 to speak to the hotel staff.

South Fork Park

Driving time:	6 minutes
Ages:	All
Length of visit:	1 hour
Directions:	Take exit 180 (US 42/US 127/Florence/Union) and head west 1.4 miles. Turn right on Farmview Drive and go 0.6 mile. Turn right on South Fork Park Drive to the park.
Cost:	Free
Hours:	Dawn–dusk
Web site:	http://www.cityofflorenceky.com/ Click on Parks and Recreation.

Description and comments: The city of Florence's South Fork Park opened in 2004 and features an outdoor playground with a soft solid rubber base. Kids can pretend to be pirates in the ship play structure. Or they can have fun on the swings and slides. The park also has a sand volleyball court, a basketball court, a drinking fountain, and a pavilion. The paved walking trail takes you to a bridge crossing a stream and through a scenic wooded area. The restroom consists of a well-maintained portable toilet with hand sanitizers (no running water). This is a great park for a short visit.

Ockerman Park

Driving time: 4 minutes

Ages: 2 and up

Length of visit: 1 hour

Directions: Take exit 180 (US 42/US 127/Florence/Union) and head west 1 mile. Turn right on Ockerman Drive. The park is on the right.

Cost: Free

Hours: Open to the public during nonschool daylight hours.

Description and comments: This park is in front of the Ockerman School campus. The old-style playground (less plastic, more metal) has a fun pretend car to drive, along with the standard swing sets, slides, and jungle gym. The base is pea gravel. There are no restrooms at this playground. Go to South Fork Park if you want a more modern playground.

Exit 178

Sports of All Sorts

Driving time:	2 minutes
Ages:	2 and up
Length of visit:	1–2 hours
Address:	10094 Investment Way, Florence, KY 41042
Directions:	Take exit 178 (KY-536/Mt. Zion Road) and head east 0.3 mile. Turn right on Investment Way. Sports of All Sorts is 0.1 mile ahead on the right.
Cost:	Bowling: $3 per game plus $1.50 shoe rental Arcade games: $0.25–$1
Hours:	Sun–Thu 10 a.m.–10 p.m., Fri 11 a.m.–11 p.m., Sat 8 a.m.–11 p.m.
Phone:	(859) 371–5511
Web site:	http://www.sportsofallsortsky.com/
Description and comments:	This Sports of All Sorts is a community recreational complex that opened in the fall of 2004. For the traveler, there is an arcade area and a bowling alley. The bowling alley is great for youngsters learning to play as well as for adults. The eight modern lanes have on-demand bumper bowling. You'll also find four nice hardwood basketball courts. These courts, depending on the time and season, may be available for open play. You can purchase food at the snack bar or play a game of pool in the bowling area. Note that there are two Sports of All Sorts locations. The same company runs them both, but each is unique. The other one is located at KY exit 181.

Kentucky Mile Marker 177

Kentucky Welcome Center

This rest area has tourist information, restrooms, telephones, vending machines, picnic tables, and space for the kids to run. Be sure to pick up a free coupon book if you are planning to stop at a hotel in Kentucky.

Cincinnati Driving

If you are heading north, you're now getting close to the Cincinnati area. Try to avoid rush hour traffic on I-75 through Cincinnati. We advise you not to drive through Cincinnati between 7 a.m. and 8:30 a.m. or between 4 p.m. and 6 p.m. on weekdays. If you must drive through the area during these times, we suggest you take I-275 west around Cincinnati. The other option is to call ARTIMIS (Advanced Regional Traffic Interactive Management & Information System) by dialing 511. After the prompts, dial 753 to get information on traffic flow from mile marker 172 in Kentucky to the Kentucky-Ohio border. You can also check traffic conditions on I-75 in Ohio and on I-275 by following the prompts. Visit http://www.artimis.org/ for further details.

Exit 175

McDonald's with an Outdoor Play Area
Big Bone Lick State Park

McDonald's with an Outdoor Play Area

Driving time: 1 minute

Directions: Take exit 175 (KY-338/Richwood) and go west 0.3 mile. McDonald's is on the right.

Big Bone Lick State Park

Driving time:	10 minutes
Ages:	All
Length of visit:	1–3 hours
Address:	3380 Beaver Road, Union, KY 41091
Directions:	Take exit 175 (KY-338/Richwood) and head west. Follow KY-338 North signs for 8 miles to the park. The park is on the left. You can follow signs to the park from I-75.
Cost:	Park: Free
	Miniature golf: $2.50
Hours:	Park: Dawn–dusk
	Museum and gift shop: 9 a.m.–5 p.m.
	Miniature golf: April 1–November 1
Phone:	(859) 384-3522
Web site:	http://www.parks.ky.gov/
Description and comments:	Big Bone Lick is an area that attracted prehistoric animals such as giant wooly mammoths, mastodons, ground sloths, and bison because of the salt and minerals found here. The mammals were driven south by ice sheets during the Ice Age and became trapped in the swamps and sulfur springs. Today, you can see a herd of live bison, walk along any of four trails, play on the playground, and visit a museum with items from an archaeological dig. Be sure to walk the Discovery Trail and view the recreated grasslands, wetlands, and wooded savannas leading to a bog, where replicas of large mammals are trapped in the muck. Miniature golf is available (follow the signs to the campground if you want to play miniature golf). Anglers in the family can try their luck from the bank of the 7.5-acre fishing lake stocked with largemouth bass, bluegills, crappie, and catfish. Be warned that the lake is on the top of a steep hill and pushing a stroller is almost

impossible. The view from the lake, especially at sunset, is beautiful. Also within the park is Big Bone Creek, which has been stocked with rainbow trout. Also available are tennis, volleyball, and basketball courts, and softball fields, horseshoe pits, and restrooms.

Wooly Mammoths

Around 4 million years ago, the first humans and wooly mammoths appeared on the earth. Humans and mammoths existed on the earth together until around 11 thousand years ago, when mammoths became extinct.

Exit 171

Walton City Park

Driving time:	4 minutes
Ages:	All
Length of visit:	1 hour
Directions:	Take exit 171 (KY-14/KY-16/Walton/Verona) and go east 0.4 mile. Turn left on School Road and go 0.5 mile. Turn left on Old Stevenson Mill Road and immediately turn right into Walton City Park.
Cost:	Free
Hours:	Dawn–dusk
Description and comments:	This is a nice community park with two separate outdoor playgrounds. One play area includes a wooden fort structure; the other has slides, swings, and climbing structures on a pea-gravel base. There are also paved walking trails, tennis courts, basketball courts, picnic areas, and restrooms. Our kids especially enjoy exploring the small creek. At this creek, our daughter discovered that crayfish have pinchers!

Exit 159

McDonald's with an Outdoor Play Area
Burger King with an Indoor Play Area

McDonald's with an Outdoor Play Area

Driving time: 1 minute

Directions: Take exit 159 (KY-22/Dry Ridge/Owenton) and go east 0.1 mile. McDonald's is on the left.

Burger King with an Indoor Play Area

Driving time: 1 minute

Directions: Take exit 159 (KY-22/Dry Ridge/Owenton) and go east 0.4 mile. Burger King is on the right.

Kentucky Mile Marker 127

Rest Area

This rest area has tourist information, public restrooms, vending machines, public telephones, and a dog walking area.

Exit 120

Kentucky Horse Park

Driving time: 2 minutes

Ages: 3 and up

Length of visit: 2–4 hours

Address: 4089 Iron Works Parkway, Lexington, KY 40511

Directions:	Take exit 120 (KY-1973/Ironworks Pike) and go east 0.8 miles. Kentucky Horse Park is on the left.
Cost:	March 15–October 31 $14 adults $7 children (ages 7–12) Free for children under 7
	November 1–March 14 $9 adults $6 children (ages 7–12) Free for children under 7
	Parking: $2
	Horseback riding: $15 (seasonal) Pony rides: $5 Christmas lights display: $15 per vehicle
Hours:	March 15–October 31: Daily 9 a.m.–5 p.m.
	November 1–March 14: Wed–Sun 9 a.m.–5 p.m.
	Closed Thanksgiving Eve, Thanksgiving Day, Christmas Eve, Christmas Day, New Year's Eve, and New Year's Day.
	The Christmas lights display (5:30 p.m.–10 p.m.) begins the Friday before Thanksgiving and continues through New Year's Eve.
Phone:	(800) 678-8813
Web site:	http://www.kyhorsepark.com/
Description and comments:	This park is a horse lover's dream. Kentucky Horse Park is a working horse farm of 1,200 acres surrounded by 30 miles of white plank fencing. The park features the American Saddlebred Museum, the International Museum of the Horse, two theaters, and nearly 50 different breeds of horse. When you arrive, go to the Visitors Information Center. Here you can pay your admission, buy tickets for horse or pony rides, obtain a schedule and map, and watch the

23-minute film *Thou Shall Fly Without Wings*. This film serves as an introduction to the world of the horse, to which the park is dedicated. Kids under 12 years old will enjoy the pony rides and playing on the large outdoor playground near the pony-ride area. Kids will also enjoy the horse-drawn tour, which is a 10-minute narrated carriage ride though the park (our kids were thrilled that the two Clydesdales pulling our carriage were named Thunder and Lightning!). Horseback rides provide visitors over 4 feet tall with a 45-minute guided trail ride through the countryside around the park. Keep in mind that all activities are open mid-March–October, but limited activities (generally the museums, galleries, and film) are available the remainder of the year. This is a must-stop if you have any horse lovers in your family.

Exit 113

Explorium of Lexington

Driving time:	10 minutes
Ages:	All
Length of visit:	2–3 hours
Address:	440 West Short Street, Lexington, KY 40507
Directions:	Take exit 113 (US 27/US 68/Paris/Lexington) and head west toward Lexington for 3 miles. Turn left on West Short Street and immediately turn right into the Victorian Square garage. After you park, take the walkway (from garage level 3) to Victorian Square. The Explorium of Lexington is on the second floor in Victorian Square.
Cost:	$5
	Free for children under 1
	Parking: 3 hours free in the Victorian Square garage with a validation stamp from the museum

Walk on the Moon exhibit at the Explorium of Lexington

Hours:	Tue–Sat 10 a.m.–5 p.m., Sun 1 p.m.–5 p.m.
	Closed New Year's Day, Easter, the week after Labor Day, Thanksgiving Day, Christmas Eve, and Christmas Day.
Phone:	(859) 258-3256
Web site:	http://www.explorium.com/
Description and comments:	This is a fun children's museum with numerous hands-on exhibits. Kids can pretend to be doctors, see a dinosaur skull replica, ride on a life-size pretend horse, walk on the moon, dance on a giant piano, and even sit in a real F–16 jet cockpit. There is a place for kids under 3 years old, where they can slide down a tree slide, sit in a bird's nest, and get wet playing at the water table without the bigger kids. Our kids really enjoyed changing water flows and creating mountains with the walnut-shell water play area (you may want to avoid this museum if anyone in your group is allergic to nuts). They also loved rolling balls on the gravity well. The biggest hit with our family was the Bubble Zone, where you have fun making huge bubbles. You can even make a bubble ring around yourself.

Looking for a Hotel?

Our favorite hotel near Lexington is the Hampton Inn just west of KY exit 110. For about $100, we received a clean room, access to an 83-degree-Fahrenheit heated indoor pool, and a continental breakfast. This hotel is a three (out of five) diamond AAA-rated hotel. Call (859) 299–2613 to speak to the hotel staff.

Exit 110

Chuck E. Cheese

Driving time:	9 minutes
Ages:	2–12
Length of visit:	1–2 hours
Address:	1555 New Circle Road, Lexington, KY 40509
Directions:	Take exit 110 (US 60/Lexington) west toward US 60 and Lexington and go 1.8 miles. Turn left on KY-4 south/New Circle Road and go 1.7 miles. Chuck E. Cheese is on the left in the Woodhill Circle Plaza.
Cost:	Admission: Free
	Arcade tokens: $0.25 (all games one token)
Hours:	Sun–Thu 9 a.m.–10 p.m., Fri–Sat 9 a.m.–11 p.m.
Phone:	(859) 268–1800
Web site:	http://www.chuckecheese.com/
Description and comments:	Kids can play child-appropriate arcade games, crawl around in a climbing play area, or watch Chuck E. Cheese and his band play music. There's even a toddler zone with special games for the smallest players. If you get hungry, you can purchase pizza, sandwiches, and salads. This Chuck E. Cheese has a Kid Check program, in which a staff member stamps your group's hands for identification. To make sure kids leave with the group they came with, a staff member checks their hand stamps as they exit. We like going to

Chuck E. Cheese for driving stops as they are generally clean, safe, and give the kids a fun place to blow off steam while their parents relax.

Exit 108

Chick-Fil-A with an Indoor Play Area
Wendy's/KFC/Pizza Hut with an Indoor Play Area

Chick-Fil-A with an Indoor Play Area

Driving time: 1 minute

Directions: Take exit 108 (Man O'War Boulevard) and go west 0.3 mile. Chick-Fil-A is on the left.

Comment: Chick-Fil-A restaurants are closed on Sunday.

Wendy's/KFC/Pizza Hut with an Indoor Play Area

Driving time: 1 minute

Directions: Take exit 108 (Man O'War Boulevard) and go west 0.2 mile. Turn left on Pleasant Ridge Boulevard. The restaurants are on the immediate left.

Exit 95

Fort Boonesborough State Park

Driving time: 8 minutes

Ages: All. The fort is best for ages 6 and up.

Length of visit: 1–3 hours

Address: 4375 Boonesboro Road, Richmond, KY 40475

Directions:	Take exit 95 (KY-627/Winchester/Boonesborough) and head east 6 miles to the entrance of Fort Boonesborough State Park. The park is on the right. Note that a separate entrance to the fort and museum is located just before the park entrance as you head east on KY-627.
Cost:	Park: Free
	Fort (includes the Kentucky River Museum): April–October $6 adults $4 children (ages 6–12) Free for children under 6
	November–March $2 adults $1 children (ages 6–12) Free for children under 6
	Pool: $4 adults $3 children (ages 3–12) Free for children under 3
	Miniature golf: $3.50 adults $2.50 children (ages 12 and under)
Hours:	Park: Daily 8 a.m.–9p.m.
	Closed major holidays
	Fort: April–October, Daily 9 a.m.–5:30 p.m.
	November–March, Wed–Sun 10 a.m.–4 p.m.
	Pool: Memorial Day–early August Daily 10:30 a.m.–6 p.m.
	Mid-August–Labor Day weekend Weekends 10:30 a.m.–6 p.m.
	Miniature golf: April 1–October 31
Phone:	(859) 527-3131
Web site:	http://www.parks.ky.gov/

Description and **comments:**	Fort Boonesborough State Park is the site of Boonesborough, established in 1775 by Richard Henderson and Daniel Boone. Today, Fort Boonesborough has been reconstructed as a working fort, complete with blockhouses, cabins, and furnishings from the late 1700s. Resident artisans perform pioneer craft demonstrations and share pioneer experiences with visitors. (We enjoyed watching candle dipping.) Older kids and adults will enjoy learning about the amazing history of the site and of Daniel Boone's family. For those who want to learn more about the area, be sure to check out the Kentucky River Museum. Here you can learn about the history of the river and how dams and locks operate.

At the park, which has a driving entrance separate from that of the fort, the family can enjoy a playground with swings, a basketball court, and a miniature golf course. On a hot summer day, visit the pool area that features a junior Olympic-size swimming pool, a water slide, a misty fountain, a children's area, and a rain tree. You can also purchase your favorite treats from the snack bar.

Exit 87

Galaxy Bowling Center

Driving time:	2 minutes
Ages:	2 and up
Length of visit:	1 hour
Address:	1025 Amberly Way, Richmond, KY 40475
Directions:	Take exit 87 (KY-876/Richmond) and go west 0.1 mile. Turn left on Amberly Way and go 0.2 mile. Galaxy Bowling Center is on the left.
Cost:	Bowling: $3.50 plus $2 for shoe rental

Hours:	Mon, Fri, and Sat 10 a.m.–1 a.m. Tue–Wed 9 a.m.–midnight Thu 10 a.m.–1 a.m. Sun noon–11 p.m.
Phone:	(859) 624-4444
Web site:	http://www.galaxybowling.com/
Description and comments:	If you and your family enjoy bowling, this modern bowling alley is a great place for a quick stop. We were surprised that bumper bowling rails came up automatically on our lane after we pushed buttons on the keypad. We were also surprised that our daughter, who was just under 3 years old at the time, was old enough to bumper bowl. After bowling, you can play games in the arcade or grab a bite to eat at the snack bar.

Kentucky Mile Marker 83

Rest Area

This rest area has restrooms, vending machines, telephones, picnic tables, and space for the kids to run.

Exit 77

Kentucky Artisan Center at Berea

Driving time:	2 minutes
Ages:	All
Length of visit:	1 hour
Address:	975 Walnut Meadow Road, Berea, KY 40403
Directions:	Take exit 77 (KY-595/Berea) and go east 0.5 mile. The Kentucky Artisan Center is on the right.

(Photo courtesy of Kentucky Artisan Center at Berea)

Cost:	Free
Hours:	8 a.m.–8 p.m.
	Closed Thanksgiving Day, Christmas Day, and New Year's Day.
Phone:	(859) 985-5448
Web site:	http://www.kentuckyartisancenter.ky.gov/
Description and comments:	At the Kentucky Artisan Center at Berea, you can shop for Kentucky-made arts and crafts, see artisan demonstrations, purchase food at the café and grill, or use the full-service rest area facilities.

Exit 76

McDonald's with an Indoor Play Area

Driving time:	1 minute
Directions:	Take exit 76 (KY-21/Berea) and go east 0.2 mile. McDonald's is on the right.

Exit 62

McDonald's with an Indoor Play Area

Driving time: 1 minute

Directions: Take exit 62 (US 25/Renfro Valley/Mount Vernon) and go east 0.2 mile to McDonald's.

Exit 38

Levi Jackson Wilderness Road State Park
McDonald's with an Indoor Play Area
Burger King with an Outdoor Play Area

Levi Jackson Wilderness Road State Park

Driving time: 10 minutes

Ages: All

Length of visit: 1–4 hours

Address: 998 Levi Jackson Mill Road, London, KY 40744

Directions: Take exit 38 (KY-192/London) and head east 2 miles. Turn right on US 25S and go 1.4 miles. Turn left on KY-1006/Levi Jackson Mill Road and go 1 mile. Turn right on Camp Area Road to Levi Jackson Wilderness Road State Park. You can follow brown signs to the park from I-75.

Cost: Park: Free

Mountain Life Museum:
$3.50 adults
$2.50 children (ages 3–12)
Free for children under 3

Pool:
$5 adults
$4 seniors (ages 62 and up)
$4 children (ages 3–12)
Free for children under 3

Miniature golf:
$3.50 adults
$2.50 children (ages 3–12)
Free for children under 3

Hours: Park: Dawn–dusk

Mountain Life Museum:
April–October, daily 9 a.m.–5 p.m.

Pool:
Memorial Day–early August
Daily noon–7:30 p.m.

Mid-August–Labor Day
Weekends noon–7:30 p.m.

Miniature golf is available April–October.

Phone: (606) 878-8000

Web site: http://www.parks.ky.gov/

Description and   Levi Jackson Wilderness Road State Park is
comments: named after both the first judge in Laurel
County and the road that over 200,000 pio-
neers traveled during the settlement of
Kentucky. You can retrace the footsteps of the
early pioneers on 1.5 miles of hiking trails. The
800-acre park includes the Defeated Camp Pio-
neer Burial Ground, which is the site of the
largest Indian massacre in Kentucky, and the
Mountain Life Museum, where you can learn
about the life of early pioneers. Cool off on a
hot summer day in the community swimming
pool, complete with water slides and a zero-
depth-entry children's pool. Adjacent to the
swimming pool, the kids can play on one of
the three playgrounds. Horseshoe pits, volleyball courts, basketball courts, and an 18-hole
miniature golf course round out the family
activities at this state park. Picnic tables and
grills are located throughout the park.

McDonald's with an Indoor Play Area

Driving time: 3 minutes

Directions: Take exit 38 (KY-192/London) and head east 1.7
                       miles. McDonald's is on the right.

Comment: This indoor play area is larger than most.

Burger King with an Outdoor Play Area

Driving time: 2 minutes

Directions: Take exit 38 (KY-192/London) and go east 0.5
                       mile. Burger King is on the left.

EXIT

Exit 29

Burger King with an Outdoor Play Area
KFC Museum

Burger King with an Outdoor Play Area

Driving time: 1 minute

Directions: Take exit 29 (US 25/US 25E/Corbin) and go east
                       0.1 mile. Burger King is on the right.

KFC Museum

Driving time: 5 minutes

Ages: All

Length of visit: 1 hour

Directions: Take exit 29 (US 25/US 25E/Corbin) and head
                       east 1.3 miles. Turn right on US 25W and go 0.5
                       mile. The KFC Museum is on the right.

Cost: Admission: Free

                      Food can be purchased.

Hours: 10 a.m.–10 p.m.

Phone: (606) 528–2163.

Description and comments: Enjoy a meal in the Colonel's original dining room and view Harland Sanders exhibits. Folks come from all over just to "eat where it all began."

Exit 25

McDonald's with an Indoor Play Area

Driving time: 1 minute

Directions: Take exit 25 (US 25W/Corbin) and go east 0.1 mile. McDonald's is on the right.

Exit 11

McDonald's with an Indoor Play Area
Hal Rogers Family Entertainment Center/
Kentucky Splash Water Park
Burger King with an Indoor Play Area

McDonald's with an Indoor Play Area

Driving time: 1 minute

Directions: Take exit 11 (KY-92/Williamsburg) and go east 0.2 mile to McDonald's.

Hal Rogers Family Entertainment Center/ Kentucky Splash Water Park

Driving time: 2 minutes

Ages: All

Length of visit: 2–4 hours

(Photo courtesy of Hal Rogers Entertainment Center)

Address: 1050 Highway 92 West, Williamsburg, KY 40769

Directions: Take exit 11 (KY-92/Williamsburg) and go west
                    0.5 mile. Hal Rogers Family Entertainment
                    Center is on the right.

Cost: Water park:
                    $14.95 adults
                    $12.95 children (ages 3–15)
                    Free for children under 3

                    An all-day activity pass that includes two go-kart
                    rides, unlimited miniature golf, two batting cage
                    tokens, and water park admission can be pur-
                    chased for $24.95.

                    The non–water park activities can also be pur-
                    chased separately. Expect to pay $2–$6 for each
                    non–water park activity.

Hours: Water park:
                    Memorial Day–early August
                    Mon–Sat 11 a.m.–7 p.m., Sun 12:30 p.m.–6 p.m.

                    Mid-August–Labor Day
                    Sat 11 a.m.–7 p.m., Sun 12:30 p.m.–6 p.m.

	Family Entertainment Center (non–water park activities): May–September, Mon–Sat noon–8 p.m., Sun 12:30 p.m.–6:30 p.m.
Phone:	(866) 812–1860
Web site:	http://www.kentuckysplash.com/
Description and comments:	If you want to cool off from a hot day of driving, this is a great place to stop. Just 2 minutes from I-75, Hal Rogers Family Entertainment Center is the largest family entertainment center in the state of Kentucky. The center is home to the Kentucky Splash Water Park, where you will find an 18,000-square-foot wave pool (with 3- to 6-foot-waves), a drift river, a children's pool, and three big water slides. Toddlers will love the small slides and dump buckets at the shallow (less than a foot deep) 6,000-square-foot children's pool. Non–water activities include go-kart rides, miniature golf, arcade games, batting cages, and a driving range. When you get hungry, you can get food (burgers, hot dogs, etc.) at the snack bar.

Burger King with an Indoor Play Area

Driving time:	2 minutes
Directions:	Take exit 11 (KY-92/Williamsburg) and go west 0.2 mile. Burger King is on the left.

Kentucky Mile Marker 2

Kentucky Welcome Center (*northbound only*)

This rest area has restrooms, picnic tables, telephones, and free 24-hour reservation phones. Be sure to pick up a free coupon book if you are planning to stop at a hotel in Kentucky.

CHAPTER
FIVE

Tennessee

Top Tennessee Family Stops

Norris Dam State Park
The Lost Sea
Mayfield Dairy Farms
Creative Discovery Museum
Tennessee Aquarium

Tennessee Quick View

Attraction	Tennessee Exit Number
Zoo or Aquarium	107A/I-40 east, 2
Park	160, 134, 128, 373 (I-40/I-75), 49
Museum	122, 107A/I-40 east, 2
Mall	380 (I-40/I-75), 5/4A
Family Entertainment Center	379A/379 (I-40/I-75), 378 (I-40/I-75), 373 (I-40/I-75)
Rest Area Mile Marker	161 (southbound only), 46, 1 (northbound only)
Fast Food with an Indoor Play Area	129, 122, 112, 379A/379 (I-40/I-75), 374 (I-40/I-75), 11
Fast Food with an Outdoor Play Area	122, 108, 72, 60, 49, 25, 1/1B
Other Attraction	378 (I-40/I-75), 60, 52

Tennessee Emergency Information

Emergency Phone:	911
Tennessee Highway Patrol Cell:	*THP (*847)
Exits with Police Sign:	none
Exits with Hospital Sign:	160, 134, 378 (I-40/I-75), 60, 49, 25

Tennessee Mile Marker 161

Tennessee Welcome Center (*southbound only*)

This welcome center has travel information, public restrooms, public telephones, vending machines, a picnic area, and space for the kids to run. Be sure to pick up a free coupon book if you are planning to stop at a hotel in Tennessee.

Exit 160

Indian Mountain State Park

Driving time:	5 minutes
Ages:	All
Length of visit:	1–2 hours
Address:	143 State Park Circle, Jellico, TN 37762
Directions:	Take exit 160 (US 25W/Jellico), and head west off the exit. Go 1.2 miles north on US 25. At the fork in the road, continue straight on West SR 297 for 0.3 mile. Turn right on London Avenue and go 0.1 mile. Turn left on Dairy Street to Indian Mountain State Park.
Cost:	Park: Free
	Pool: $3
	Free for children under 2
Hours:	Park: 7 a.m.–dusk
	Park office: 8 a.m.–4:30 p.m.
	Pool: Labor Day–mid-August, 10 a.m.–6 p.m.
Phone:	(423) 784-7958
Web site:	http://www.state.tn.us/environment
	Click on the State Parks logo.

Description and comments: Located at the base of Indian Mountain, Indian Mountain State Park is a good place to stretch your legs and enjoy the outdoors. This 200-acre park is unique in that it was developed on reclaimed strip-mine land. Park visitors can enjoy fishing at the two small lakes. Restrooms, picnic tables, pedal boats, hiking trails (one paved, one not paved), and an outdoor swimming pool are also available. You can also enjoy several small outdoor playgrounds, with seesaws, monkey bars, swings, and slides for the kids. We saw plenty of wildlife, including a large flock of geese, during one visit. If you want to visit a Tennessee state park but don't enjoy the hilly terrain that some of the others have, this is a good stop for you.

Exit 134

Cove Lake State Park

Driving time: 3 minutes

Ages: All

Length of visit: 1–3 hours

Address: 110 Cove Lake Lane, Caryville, TN 37714

Directions: Take exit 134 (US 25W/TN-63/Caryville), and go east 0.5 mile. Take the first left turn to the entrance of Cove Lake State Park.

Cost: $3 per vehicle
Pool: $3
Free for children under 2

Hours:	Park: 8 a.m.–dusk
	Pool:
	Memorial Day weekend–Labor Day, 11 a.m.–7 p.m. However, starting August 1, the pool is open only when local lifeguards are available. It is best to call ahead if you plan to use the pool.
Phone:	(423) 566-9701
Web site:	http://www.state.tn.us/environment Click on the State Parks logo.
Description and comments:	If you want to visit a Tennessee state park but don't want to venture far from I-75, this one is for you. Cove Lake State Park's 673 acres are situated in a beautiful mountain valley on the eastern edge of the Cumberland Mountains, a half mile from I-75. You can take a walk or hike on the nature trails (including paved trails); play badminton, shuffleboard, horseshoes, volleyball, Ping-Pong, or tennis; or choose from many other activities. The park also has playgrounds for kids to enjoy and an outdoor swimming pool. Anglers can try their luck fishing from the bank and bridges near the entrance. Recreation equipment is available on a free checkout system at the boat dock in the summer months or in the park office during the remainder of the year. Restrooms are available.

Knoxville Driving

If you are heading south, you're now getting close to the Knoxville area. Because of construction along I-40/I-75, we advise you to avoid driving through Knoxville between 6:30 a.m. and 9 a.m. and between 4 p.m. and 7 p.m. on weekdays. Visit http://www.tdot.state.tn.us/ and click on State Map–Construction/Incident Information to get updated information prior to your trip. Or call the construction hotline at (800) 858-6349 to obtain the latest construction information.

Exit 129

McDonald's with an Indoor Play Area
Burger King with an Indoor Play Area

McDonald's with an Indoor Play Area

Driving time: 1 minute

Directions: Take exit 129 (US 25W/Lake City) and go west 0.1 mile. McDonald's is on the left.

Burger King with an Indoor Play Area

Driving time: 1 minute

Directions: Take exit 129 (US 25W/Lake City) and go west 0.1 mile. Burger King is on the right.

Exit 128

Norris Dam State Park

Driving time: 5 minutes

Ages: 2 and up

Length of visit: 1–4 hours

Address: 125 Village Green Circle, Lake City, TN 37769

Directions: Take exit 128 (US 441/Lake City) and head east off the exit. Go 2.5 miles south on US 441 to Norris Dam State Park. Directions are signed from I-75.

Cost: Park: Free

Pool: $2.50
Free for children under 2

Hours:	Park: Dawn–10 p.m.
	Park Office: 8 a.m.–4:30 p.m.
	Pool:
	Memorial Day weekend–Labor Day, 10 a.m.–6 p.m. However, starting August 1, the pool is open only when local lifeguards are available. It is best to call ahead if you plan to use the pool.
Phone:	Park: (865) 426-7461
	Museum: (865) 494-9688
Web site:	http://www.state.tn.us/environment
	Click on the State Parks logo.
Description and comments:	Located on Norris Reservoir, this 4,000-acre park is another Tennessee jewel. Stop and let the kids expend some energy and enjoy the scenery surrounding the reservoir. Or get involved in an activity such as tennis, badminton, basketball, horseshoes, or volleyball. Equipment for these activities may be checked out at the park office. Also available are restrooms, a small playground, hiking trails (hilly!), facilities for boating (pontoons can be rented), fishing, picnicking, and seasonal swimming in the outdoor pool. Be sure to take a scenic drive across Norris Dam. If you are interested in this area's history, visit the museum complex with Appalachian artifacts. School-age kids and older should find the museum interesting, but there are no hands-on activities for younger kids.

Tennessee Trivia

- Elvis Presley's home, Graceland, is located in Memphis. Graceland is the second most visited house in the country.
- Tennessee became the 16th state in 1796.
- The Great Smoky Mountains National Park is the most visited national park in the United States. The park was named for the smoke-like bluish haze that often envelops the mountains.

Exit 122

The Museum of Appalachia
McDonald's with an Outdoor Play Area
Burger King with an Indoor Play Area

The Museum of Appalachia

Driving time:	2 minutes
Ages:	6 and up
Length of visit:	1–3 hours
Address:	2819 Andersonville Highway Clinton, TN 37716
Directions:	Take exit 122 (TN-61/Norris/Clinton) and head east 1 mile. The museum is on the left.
Cost:	$12.95 adults $10 seniors (ages 65 and up) $5 children (ages 6–12) Free for children under 6
Hours:	8 a.m.–about 1 hour before dusk (5 p.m. in the winter and 8 p.m. in the summer) Call for the current closing time. Closed Christmas Day.
Phone:	(865) 494-7680
Web site:	http://www.museumofappalachia.com/
Description and comments:	The Museum of Appalachia has been called the most authentic and complete replica of pioneer Appalachian life in the world. Visitors can see spinning and weaving, replicas of schools and chapels, and Mark Twain's family cabin. You can purchase locally made arts and crafts, enjoy some home-cooked food, and watch farm animals roam. We enjoyed relaxing on the rocking chairs on the porch and watching the sheep graze. Anyone interested in music, especially stringed instruments, should enjoy the musical instruments section. School-age kids and

older should enjoy learning about this way of life. There are no hands-on activities for toddlers and preschoolers. This place is a real step back in time and an enjoyable and relaxing way to spend a couple of hours.

Looking for a Hotel?

Our favorite hotel on the north side of Knoxville is the Country Inn & Suites just east of TN exit 112. For under $70 (Internet rate), we received a clean room with two double beds, access to a heated indoor pool, and a continental breakfast. Plus we enjoyed raiding the fruit and cookie jars after an evening swim. This hotel is a three (out of five) diamond AAA-rated hotel. Call (865) 947-7500 to speak to the hotel staff.

McDonald's with an Outdoor Play Area

Driving time: 1 minute

Directions: Take exit 122 (TN-61/Norris/Clinton) and go west 0.2 mile. McDonald's is on the right.

Burger King with an Indoor Play Area

Driving time: 1 minute

Directions: Take exit 122 (TN-61/Norris/Clinton) and go west 0.1 mile. Burger King is on the left.

Exit 112

McDonald's with an Indoor Play Area

Driving time: 1 minute

Directions: Take exit 112 (TN-131/Emory Road/Powell) and go east 0.4 mile. McDonald's is on the left.

Comment: This play area includes a kid-size air hockey table and four Nintendo Playstations with kid-appropriate games.

Exit 108

McDonald's with an Outdoor Play Area

Driving time:	1 minute
Directions:	Take exit 108 (Merchant Drive) and go west 0.2 mile. McDonald's is on the left.
Comment:	This McDonald's is open 24 hours a day.

Exit 107A or I-40 East

Knoxville Zoo
East Tennessee Discovery Center

Knoxville Zoo

Driving time:	10 minutes
Ages:	All
Length of visit:	3 hours
Address:	3500 Knoxville Zoo Drive, Knoxville, TN 37914
Directions heading south:	Take exit 107A (I-275). Immediately take I-275 exit 3 (I-640 east). Head east on I-640 for 7 miles. Take I-40 west and go 1 mile. Take I-40 exit 392A (Rutledge Pike) and follow the signs to the Knoxville Zoo.
Directions heading north:	Heading north toward Knoxville on I-40/I-75, stay on I-40 east toward Knoxville. Note that I-75 merges with I-640 at exit 385: stay on I-40 here, not I-75/I-640. Head east on I-40 for 7 miles. Take I-40 exit 392 (to US 11W south) and follow the signs to the Knoxville Zoo.
Cost:	$12.95 adults $8.95 seniors (ages 62 and up) $8.95 children (ages 3–12) Free for children under 3 Admission is half price December–February.

Parking: $3

Stroller rentals: $6

Camel rides: $3

Burro rides: $3
(you must be 42 inches or shorter to ride)

This zoo is a member of AZA.

Hours: Hours are variable, call or see the Web site before you visit.

General hours:
Mid-October–Mid-March
Daily 10 a.m.–4:30 p.m.

Mid-March–May
Mon–Fri 9:30 a.m.–4:30 p.m.,
Weekends 9:30 a.m.–6 p.m.

June–August
Daily 9:30 a.m.–6 p.m.

September–mid-October
Mon–Fri 9:30 a.m.–4:30 p.m.,
Weekends 9:30 a.m.–6 p.m.

Closed Christmas Day.

Phone: (865) 637–5331

Web site: http://www.knoxville-zoo.org/

The river otter exhibit at the Knoxville Zoo (Photo courtesy of the Knoxville Zoo)

Description and comments:	Stop at the Knoxville Zoo and visit reptiles, otters, white rhinos, red pandas, zebras, tigers, and African elephants. We especially enjoyed the views of the elephants, zebras, and chimps. In the children's zoo area, crawl through a pretend prairie dog tunnel or take seasonal burro or camel rides. In April 2005, the zoo opened KidsCove. Here kids can cool off in a wet play area, climb and slide in a giant playground, climb a rock wall, milk a pretend cow, or pretend to be a zookeeper. This area is designed to please kids 3–10 years of age.

East Tennessee Discovery Center

Driving time:	11 minutes
Ages:	2–10
Length of visit:	1–2 hours
Address:	516 North Beaman Street, Knoxville, TN 37914
Directions heading south:	Take exit 107A (I-275). Immediately take I-275 exit 3 (I-640 east). Head east on I-640 for 7 miles. Take I-40 west and go 1 mile. Take I-40 exit 392A (Rutledge Pike) and go 0.7 mile. Rutledge Pike merges with East Magnolia Avenue. Go straight on East Magnolia Avenue 0.5 mile. Turn right on North Beaman Street. The East Tennessee Discovery Center is on the right.
Directions heading north:	Heading north toward Knoxville on I-40/I-75, stay on I-40 east toward Knoxville. Note that I-75 merges with I-640 at exit 385: stay on I-40 here, not I-75/I-640. Head east on I-40 5 miles. Take I-40 exit 390 to Cherry Street. Turn right on Cherry Street and go 0.3 mile. Turn left on Woodbine Avenue and go 0.8 mile. Go straight on North Beaman Street to the East Tennessee Discovery Center.

Cost:	$4 adults $3 seniors (ages 55 and up) $3 children (ages 5–18) $2 toddlers (ages 3 and 4) Free for children under 3 Parking: Free This museum is a member of ASTC and ACM.
Hours:	Mon–Fri 9 a.m.–5 p.m., Sat 10 a.m.–5 p.m. Closed most holidays.
Phone:	(865) 594–1494
Web site:	http://www.etdiscovery.org/
Description and comments:	The East Tennessee Discovery Center is a small but fun science museum. It's perfect for a 1- to 2-hour stop to let the kids run around, have fun, and learn something at the same time. Visit the Life Science area, where you can observe live fish, snakes, lizards, and turtles. Or look through a microscope at a large collection of preserved insects, a tarantula, and even a bee colony (see if you can find the queen bee!). In the Physical Science area, kids can learn about light and vision, sound, simple machines, and energy. Our kids liked using a crane to lift things, using a digger to move around soft "rocks," and building a maze of pipes and then racing balls through them. In the Earth Science area, kids can touch fossils and rocks. Then they can pretend they are astronauts and drive the almost life-size Discovery Space Shuttle complete with outer space–sounding controls. There is also a Kidspace area where kids aged 2–7 can play educational computer games, build Lego masterpieces, and dress up, all at their own pace. Our kids enjoyed building and racing Lego racecars in this area.

Exit 380 (I-40/I-75)

West Town Mall

Driving time:	2 minutes
Ages:	2 and up
Length of visit:	1–2 hours
Address:	7600 Kingston Pike, Knoxville, TN 37919
Directions:	Take I-40/I-75 exit 380 (US 11/US 70/West Hills) and go east 0.2 mile. Turn right on Morrell Road and then turn right into the mall entrance.
Cost:	Free
Hours:	Mon–Sat 10 a.m.–9 p.m., Sun 12:30 p.m.–6 p.m.
Phone:	(865) 693-0292
Web site:	http://www.simon.com/
Description and comments:	Stop and take a leisurely walk through the West Town Mall. You will find something to satisfy your appetite at one of the 12 restaurants in the food court. Or do some shopping at any of over 150 stores, including Sears, Dillard's, JCPenney, Proffitt's, and Parisian. Toddlers and preschoolers will enjoy the small coin-operated rides. Older kids may want to visit the arcade located near the movie theater.

Exit 379A or 379 (I-40/I-75)

Chuck E. Cheese
Burger King with an Indoor Play Area

Chuck E. Cheese

Driving time:	4 minutes

Ages:	2–12
Length of visit:	1–2 hours
Address:	8225 Kingston Pike, Knoxville, TN 37919
Directions heading south:	Take I-40/I-75 exit 379A (Gallaher View Drive). Turn left on Gallaher View Drive and go 0.2 mile. Turn left on Kingston Pike and go 0.2 mile. Chuck E. Cheese is on the left.
Directions heading north:	Take exit 379 (Bridgewater/Walker Springs Road/ Gallaher View Drive). Turn right on Walker Springs Road and go 0.1 mile. Turn left on Kingston Pike and go 0.6 mile. Chuck E. Cheese is on the left.
Cost:	Admission: Free
	Arcade tokens: $0.25 (all games one token)
Hours:	Sun–Thu 9 a.m.–10 p.m.,
	Fri–Sat 9 a.m.–11 p.m.
Phone:	(865) 670-8586
Web site:	http://www.chuckecheese.com/
Description and comments:	Kids can play child-appropriate arcade games, crawl around in a climbing play area, or watch Chuck E. Cheese and his band play music. There's even a toddler zone with special games for the smallest players. If you get hungry, you can purchase pizza, sandwiches, and salads. This Chuck E. Cheese has a Kid Check program, in which a staff member stamps your group's hands for identification. To make sure kids leave with the group they came with, a staff member checks their hand stamps as they exit. We like going to Chuck E. Cheese for driving stops as they are generally clean, safe, and give the kids a fun place to blow off steam while their parents relax.

Burger King with an Indoor Play Area

Driving time:	2 minutes
Directions heading south:	Take exit 379A (Gallaher View Drive). Turn left on Gallaher View Drive and go 0.2 mile. Turn right on Kingston Pike and go 0.1 mile. Burger King is on the left.
Directions heading north:	Take exit 379 (Bridgewater/Walker Springs Road/Gallaher View Drive). Turn right on Walker Springs Road and go 0.1 mile. Turn left on Kingston Pike and go 0.3 mile. Burger King is on the right.

Exit 378 (I-40/I-75)
Zuma Fun Center
Family Bowl

Zuma Fun Center

Driving time:	3 minutes
Ages:	2 and up
Length of visit:	1–3 hours
Address:	400 North Peters Road Knoxville, TN 37922
Directions heading south:	Take I-40/I-75 exit 378 (Cedar Bluff Road). Take a slight left (exit A) at the fork toward South Cedar Bluff Road and go 0.4 mile. Turn left on North Cedar Bluff Road and go 0.3 mile. Turn right on North Peters Road and go 0.6 mile. The Zuma Fun Center is on the right.
Directions heading north:	Take I-40/I-75 exit 378 (Cedar Bluff Road). Turn right on North Cedar Bluff Road and go 0.3 mile. Turn right on North Peters Road and go 0.6 mile. The Zuma Fun Center is on the right.

Cost:	Admission: Free
	Arcade games: $0.25–$1
	Playland rides: $2–$6
	Unlimited outdoor ride passes: $20.99
Hours:	Hours are variable, so call or see the Web site before you visit.
	General hours: Memorial Day–mid-August Mon–Thu 10 a.m.–10 p.m., Fri–Sat 10 a.m.–11 p.m., Sun noon–9 p.m.
	Late August–Memorial Day Mon–Thu 4 p.m.–9 p.m., Fri 4 p.m.–11 p.m., Sat 10 a.m.–11 p.m., Sun noon–9 p.m.
Phone:	(865) 539-2288
Web site:	http://www.zumafuncenters.com/
Description and comments:	The Zuma Fun Center is an indoor and outdoor family entertainment center. The inside will remind you of Chuck E. Cheese, with an indoor arcade, restaurant, and entertainment. Outdoor activities include batting cages, bumper boats, go-karts (for kids 54 inches and taller), miniature golf, and Playland rides. These rides include a train, a swing ride, airplanes, and other rides geared toward toddlers and preschoolers. This is a great place if you like both arcade games and outdoor rides.

Knoxville Driving

If you are heading north, you're now getting close to the Knoxville area. Because of the construction along I-40/I-75, we advise you to avoid driving through Knoxville between 6:30 a.m. and 9 a.m. and between 4 p.m. and 7 p.m. on weekdays. Visit http://www.tdot.state.tn.us/ and click on State Map–Construction\Incident Information to get updated information prior to your trip. Or call the construction hotline at (800) 858-6349 to get the latest construction information.

Family Bowl

Driving time:	5 minutes
Ages:	3 and up
Directions heading south:	Take I-40/I-75 exit 378 (Cedar Bluff Road). Take a slight left (exit A) at the fork toward South Cedar Bluff Road and go 0.4 mile. Turn left on North Cedar Bluff Road and go 0.3 mile. Turn right on North Peters Road and drive 1 mile. Family Bowl is on the left.
Directions heading north:	Take I-40/I-75 exit 378 (Cedar Bluff Road). Turn right on North Cedar Bluff Road and go 0.3 mile. Turn right on North Peters Road and go 1 mile. Family Bowl is on the left.
Cost:	Bowling: $2.50–$4 per game
Hours:	Mon, Thu, Fri 11 a.m.–1 a.m. Tue–Wed, Sat 9 a.m.–1 a.m. Sun noon–1 a.m.
Phone:	(865) 690–5211
Description and comments:	As its name implies, Family Bowl is a bowling alley that offers automatic bumper bowling. There are also a few arcade games.

Exit 374 (I-40/I-75)

McDonald's with an Indoor Play Area

Driving time:	1 minute
Directions:	Take I-40/I-75 exit 374 (Lovell Road/TN-131) and go east 0.2 mile. McDonald's is on the right.

Exit 373 (I-40/I-75)

Putt-Putt Golf & Games
Campbell Station Park

Putt-Putt Golf & Games

Driving time:	6 minutes
Ages:	3 and up
Length of visit:	1–2 hours
Address:	164 West End Avenue, Farragut, TN 37922
Directions:	Take I-40/I-75 exit 373 (Campbell Station Road/ Farragut) and head east off the exit. Go southeast on Campbell Station Road 1.8 miles. Turn left on Kingston Pike and go 0.5 mile to West End Avenue. Turn left on West End Avenue. Putt-Putt Golf & Games is on the right.
Cost:	Miniature golf: $5
	Arcade game tokens: $0.25
Hours:	Hours are variable, so call or visit the Web site before you visit.
	General hours: Mid-May–Mid-August Mon–Fri 10 a.m.–10 p.m., Weekends 10 a.m.–11 p.m.
	Late August–Mid-November Mid-February–Early May Mon–Fri 2 p.m.–9 p.m., Weekends 10 a.m.–10 p.m.
Phone:	(865) 675–5558
Web site:	http://www.farragutputtputt.com/
Description and comments:	Stop and play miniature golf, hit baseballs in the batting cages, play arcade games, or hit golf balls at the driving range. In case you get hungry, there is a snack bar with pizza, hot dogs, ice cream, and other treats.

Campbell Station Park

Driving time:	3 minutes
Ages:	All
Length of visit:	1 hour
Directions:	Take I-40/I-75 exit 373 (Campbell Station Road/ Farragut) and head east off the exit. Go southeast on Campbell Station Road 0.9 mile. Campbell Station Park is on the right.
Cost:	Free
Hours:	Dawn–dusk
Web site:	http://www.townoffarragut.org/parksand recareas.html
Description and comments:	If you need a quick break from driving, this small, relaxing community park is a good place to visit. Take a walk on the paved trails. Restrooms and a pavilion are available. This is a nice park for a picnic.

Kid Trivia

Three former presidents, Andrew Jackson (1829–1837), James K. Polk (1845–1849), and Andrew Johnson (1865–1869), are from Tennessee.

Exit 72

McDonald's with an Outdoor Play Area

Driving time:	1 minute
Directions:	Take exit 72 (TN-72/Loudon) and go east 0.2 mile. McDonald's is on the right.

EXIT

Exit 60

McDonald's with an Outdoor Play Area
The Lost Sea

McDonald's with an Outdoor Play Area

Driving time: 1 minute

Directions: Take exit 60 (TN-68/Sweetwater) and go east 0.2 mile. McDonald's is on the left.

The Lost Sea

Driving time: 10 minutes

Ages: 4 and up

Length of visit: 1–3 hours

Address: 140 Lost Sea Road, Sweetwater, TN 37874

Directions: Take exit 60 (TN-68/Sweetwater) and head east 7.5 miles. The Lost Sea is on the left.

Cost: $12.95 adults
$5.95 children (ages 6–12)
Free for children under 6

Hours: November–February, 9 a.m.–5 p.m.
March–April, 9 a.m.–6 p.m.
May–June, 9 a.m.–7 p.m.
July, 9 a.m.–8 p.m.
August, 9 a.m.–7 p.m.
September–October, 9 a.m.–6 p.m.
Closed Christmas Day.

Phone: (423) 337-6616

Web site: http://www.thelostsea.com/

Description and comments:	The Lost Sea is 4.5-acre underground lake and cavern. An hour long guided tour takes you down a half-mile path through the cave to the lake. The narrator describes the cave history and geological development. During the descent, our tour guide turned off the lights to allow us to experience total darkness, which is fascinating but may be a bit intense for young children who are afraid of the dark. At the bottom, you take a short boat ride around the lake. Our favorite part of the boat ride was watching the numerous 6-pound rainbow trout devour the food the tour guide threw in the water. After the boat ride, you walk a quarter of a mile up a fairly steep incline through the cave, back to the entrance. Several families in our group were pushing strollers, but be advised that the walk back up is steep. Also, the air temperature inside the cave is 58 degrees Fahrenheit year-round, so be sure to dress appropriately. Outside the cave are authentic log cabins, which include a general store, an ice cream parlor, a trading post, and a glassblower. Food is available. There are also picnic facilities and a nature trail to enjoy. This is a fun and unique stop along I-75.

EXIT

Exit 52

Mayfield Dairy Farms

Driving time:	7 minutes
Ages:	4 and up. Ice cream eating is good for all ages!
Length of visit:	1–3 hours
Address:	4 Mayfield Lane, Athens, TN 37303
Directions:	Take exit 52 (TN-305/Athens) and head east 4.3 miles. Mayfield Dairy Farms is on the left.

Kid Trivia

Can you guess the two most popular flavors of Mayfield ice cream?
The answer: vanilla and Moosetracks.

Cost:	Tour: Free Ice cream: $1 per scoop
Hours:	Mon–Fri 9 a.m.–5 p.m., Sat 9 a.m.–2 p.m.

On Monday, Tuesday, Thursday, and Friday, tours depart every 30 minutes (there is no tour at noon). On Wednesday, tours depart every hour. There is no milk production (a major part of the tour) on Wednesday. On Saturday, tours depart every hour. There is no ice cream production on Saturday. The last tour departs one hour prior to closing.

Closed December 31–January 2, July 4, Labor Day, Thanksgiving Eve, Thanksgiving Day, and December 24–26.

Phone:	(800) 629-3435
Web site:	http://www.mayfielddairy.com/
Description and comments:	Enjoy one of the 30 flavors of the "world's best ice cream," in the words of a major magazine. Take a tour of the company's milk and ice cream production facility. The tour begins with an informative 10-minute video about the facility. Everyone then puts on a hairnet (supplied) and begins the 30-minute tour. You can watch how plastic milk jugs are made (a kid favorite!). Then you can see how the jugs are labeled, filled with milk, and capped. Also see how bottles and cartons are filled. The tour ends with a peek at the ice cream production facility. Some equipment is loud, and young children sensitive to loud noises may not enjoy the tour. Better yet, bring some earplugs just in case.

Exit 49

Burger King with an Outdoor Play Area
McDonald's with an Outdoor Play Area
Athens Regional Park

Burger King with an Outdoor Play Area

Driving time: 1 minute

Directions: Take exit 49 (TN-30/Decatur/Athens) and go east 0.1 mile. Burger King is on the right.

McDonald's with an Outdoor Play Area

Driving time: 4 minutes

Directions: Take exit 49 (TN-30/Decatur/Athens) and head east 1.8 miles. McDonald's is on the right.

Athens Regional Park

Driving time: 2 minutes

Ages: All

Length of visit: 1 hour

Directions: Take exit 49 (TN-30/Decatur/Athens) and go east 0.8 mile. Athens Regional Park is on the right.

Cost: Free

Hours: April–October, 7 a.m.–11 p.m.
November–March, 7 a.m.–10 p.m.

Phone: (423) 744-2704

Web site: http://www.cityofathenstn.com/
Click on Parks & Recreation,
then Parks & Reservations.

Description and comments: This community park has a walking trail around a small lake, mountain biking and hiking trails through a wooded area, a playground, soccer and softball fields, and restrooms. This is a great place for a quick stop.

Tennessee Mile Marker 46

Rest Area

This rest area has public restrooms, vending machines, public telephones, a picnic area, and space for kids to run.

Exit 25

McDonald's with an Outdoor Play Area
Burger King with an Outdoor Play Area

McDonald's with an Outdoor Play Area

Driving time: 1 minute

Directions: Take exit 25 (TN-60/Cleveland/Dayton) and go east 0.6 mile. McDonald's is on the left.

Burger King with an Outdoor Play Area

Driving time: 1 minute

Directions: Take exit 25 (TN-60/Cleveland/Dayton) and go east 0.6 mile. Burger King is on the right.

Exit 11

McDonald's with an Indoor Play Area
Burger King with an Indoor Play Area

McDonald's with an Indoor Play Area

Driving time: 2 minutes

Directions: Take exit 11 (US 11N/US 64E/Ooltewah) and go
east 0.4 mile. McDonald's is on the left.

Burger King with an Indoor Play Area

Driving time: 2 minutes

Directions: Take exit 11 (US 11N/US 64E/Ooltewah) and go
east 0.4 mile. Burger King is on the right.

Exit 5 or 4A

Hamilton Place Mall

Driving time: 2 minutes

Ages: 2 and up

Length of visit: 1–2 hours

Address: 2100 Hamilton Place Boulevard
Chattanooga, TN 37421

**Directions
heading south:**   Take exit 5 (Shallowford Road) and go east 0.1
mile. Turn right on Hamilton Place Boulevard to
the mall.

**Directions
heading north:**   Take exit 4A (Hamilton Place Boulevard) and
drive directly to the mall.

Cost: Free

Hours:	Mon–Sat 10 a.m.–9 p.m., Sun noon–6 p.m.
Phone:	(423) 894–7177
Web site:	http://www.hamiltonplace.com/
Description and comments:	The Hamilton Place Mall is a major mall with quick access from I-75. Hamilton Place is home to over 200 stores, including Dillard's, JCPenney, Parisian, Proffitt's, and Sears. Toddlers and preschoolers will enjoy the soft play area on the first floor near Parisian. Small coin-operated rides, a carousel, and a food court are also available for your enjoyment.

Exit 2

Creative Discovery Museum
Tennessee Aquarium

Creative Discovery Museum

Driving time:	15 minutes
Ages:	All
Length of visit:	2–4 hours
Address:	321 Chestnut Street, Chattanooga, TN 37402
Directions:	Take exit 2 (I-24 west/Chattanooga) and head west 7 miles to I-24 exit 178 (US 27 north). Go 1.5 miles north on US 27 and take US 27 exit 1C (4th Street). Merge right on 4th Street. Turn left at the first light onto Chestnut Street and go one block. Park on either side of Chestnut Street.

The Riverplay area at Creative Discovery Museum
(Photo courtesy of Creative Discovery Museum)

Cost: $7.95 adults
                   $6.95 children (ages 2–12)
                   Free for children under 2

                   Parking: $4

                   Combination ticket (Tennessee Aquarium,
                   Creative Discovery Museum, and one IMAX
                   movie): $28.50 adults
                   $18.50 children (ages 2–12)
                   Free for children under 2

                   This museum is a member of ASTC and ACM.

Hours: March–May
                   Mon–Sat 10 a.m.–5 p.m.,
                   Sun noon–5 p.m.

                   Memorial Day–Labor Day
                   Daily 10 a.m.–6 p.m.

                   September–February
                   Mon, Tue, Thu, Fri, Sat 10 a.m.–5 p.m.,
                   Sun noon–5 p.m.

                   Closed Thanksgiving Day, Christmas Eve, and
                   Christmas Day.

Phone:	(423) 756-2738
Web site:	http://www.cdmfun.org/
Description and comments:	You'll know by just looking at the outside of the Creative Discovery Museum that your kids will love this place. This children's museum has nine hands-on discovery areas. One such area includes a 60-foot tower, from which you can view downtown Chattanooga with a telescope. Kids can also dig for dinosaur bones, play music, get wet in a river play area, and explore an artist's studio. During nice weather, be sure to go to the Rooftop Fun Factory where you can launch balls, blow bubbles, and do arts and crafts on the roof. Kids under age 4 can climb in a treehouse or play in the kitchen of the Little Yellow House. There are also changing, temporary exhibits. Gifts and snacks are available. Going to both the Tennessee Aquarium and the Creative Discovery Museum is well worth the 15-minute drive to Chattanooga for our family.

Tennessee Aquarium

Driving time:	15 minutes
Ages:	All
Length of visit:	1–3 hours
Address:	One Broad Street, Chattanooga, TN 37401
Directions:	Take exit 2 (I-24 west/Chattanooga) and head west 7 miles to I-24 exit 178 (US 27 north). Go 1.5 miles north on US 27 and take US 27 exit 1C (4th Street). Merge right on 4th Street. Turn left at the second light onto Broad Street. Go two blocks to the aquarium. The aquarium is at the corner of 2nd Street and Broad Street. Turn left on 2nd Street and park on the right, or park at any local lot.

The Gulf of Mexico exhibit at the Tennessee Aquarium
(Photo by Todd Stailey courtesy of the Tennessee Aquarium)

Cost:

$17.95 adults
$9.50 children (ages 3–12)
Free for children under 3

Combination ticket (Tennessee Aquarium, Creative Discovery Museum, and one IMAX movie): $28.50 adults
$18.50 children (ages 3–12)
Free for children under 2

Parking:
$2–$6 in local garages
$5 on 2nd Street adjacent to the aquarium

This aquarium is a member of AZA.

Hours:

10 a.m.–6 p.m.
Summer hours are extended.

Closed Thanksgiving Day and Christmas Day.

Phone: (800) 262-0695

Web site: http://www.tnaqua.org/

Description and comments: Stop at this beautiful aquarium with great displays of both freshwater and saltwater fish and other animals. After a spring 2005 expansion, the aquarium is divided into two sections. The first section is the River Journey building. This is the older part of the aquarium and tells the story of the path of a raindrop from the Appalachian Forest to the Gulf of Mexico. This section is very interesting, with lots of waterfalls and animal movement. We particularly liked viewing the otters and watching scuba divers interact with us at the Gulf of Mexico exhibit. The new expansion is aptly named Ocean Journey. The centerpiece is the over–600,000-gallon saltwater reef exhibit, complete with schooling fishes and large sand tiger sharks (just look for the huge sharks with teeth protruding from their mouths!). A big hit with kids of all ages is Shark Island, where you may touch a variety of harmless sharks and stingrays. After leaving Shark Island, visit Butterfly Garden, where hundreds of free-flying butterflies will mesmerize you with their grace and beauty. Before leaving, you will get a chance to view giant Japanese spider crabs, the giant Pacific octopus, and lots of jellyfish. Our kids, and many others, seemed to enjoy the outside of the aquarium almost as much as the inside, including walking over bridges and playing in the small water spray area. Going to both the Tennessee Aquarium and the Creative Discovery Museum is well worth the 15-minute drive to Chattanooga for our family.

Tennessee Mile Marker 1

Tennessee Welcome Center (*northbound only*)

This welcome center has public restrooms, telephones, and tourist information. Be sure to pick up a free coupon book if you are planning to stop at a Tennessee hotel.

EXIT

Exit 1 or 1B
McDonald's with an Outdoor Play Area Burger King with an Outdoor Play Area

McDonald's with an Outdoor Play Area

Driving time:	1 minute
Directions heading south:	Take exit 1 (US 41/East Ridge) and go west 0.2 mile. McDonald's is on the right.
Directions heading north:	Take exit 1B (US 41 N/East Ridge) and go west 0.2 mile. McDonald's is on the right.

Burger King with an Outdoor Play Area

Driving time:	1 minute
Directions heading south:	Take exit 1 (US 41/East Ridge) and go west 0.2 mile. Burger King is on the left.
Directions heading north:	Take exit 1B (US 41 N/East Ridge) and go west 0.2 mile. Burger King is on the left.

CHAPTER
S I X

Georgia

Top Georgia Family Stops

Red Top Mountain State Park
Imagine It! The Children's Museum of Atlanta
World of Coca-Cola
Reed Bingham State Park
Wild Adventures

Georgia Quick View

Attraction	Georgia Exit Number
Zoo or Aquarium	247
Park	350, 288, 285, 269, 250, 249C/248C, 198, 63A, 39
Museum	293, 273, 249C/248C, 9 (I-475)
Mall	269, 258, 233, 5 (I-475), 18
Family Entertainment Center	269, 261, 258, 5 (I-475)
Rest Area Mile Marker	Southbound only: 353, 320, 179, 118, 76, 48 Northbound only: 308, 8 (I-475), 108, 85, 48, 3
Fast Food with an Indoor Play Area	348, 333, 312, 273, 269, 7 (I-285), 255, 231, 221, 218, 212, 9 (I-475), 136, 101, 63A, 62, 39, 22, 18, 5
Fast Food with an Outdoor Play Area	290, 277, 273, 269, 60 (I-285), 218, 187, 149, 136, 101, 82, 63A, 62, 39, 18, 16, 5
Other Attraction	265, 10B (I-285), 248A/246, 63B, 62, 13

Georgia Emergency Information

Emergency Phone:	911
Georgia Highway Patrol Cell:	*477
Exits with Police Sign:	336, 312, 293, 271, 185, 135, 121, 101, 11
Exits with Hospital Sign:	350, 336, 315, 290, 267B, 7 (I-285), 255, 252B, 249D, 241, 235, 224, 187, 9 (I-475) 146, 138, 102, 63B, 39, 22

Georgia Mile Marker 353

Georgia Welcome Center (*southbound only*)

The visitor center is open 8 a.m.–5:30 p.m. and restrooms are open 7 a.m.–10 p.m. You will also find telephones, vending machines, and space for kids to run. Be sure to pick up a free coupon book if you are planning to stop at a hotel in Georgia.

Exit 350

Chickamauga Battlefield National Military Park

Driving time:	13 minutes
Ages:	10 and up
Length of visit:	1–3 hours
Address:	3370 Lafayette Road Fort Oglethorpe, GA 30742
Directions:	Take exit 350 (GA-2/Battlefield Parkway/Fort Oglethorpe) and head west 7.4 miles. Turn left on Lafayette Road and drive 1 mile to the park entrance. The visitor center is on the right.
Cost:	Park: Free Movie (*The Battle of Chickamauga*): $3 adults $1.50 children (ages 12 and younger)
Hours:	8:30 a.m.–5 p.m. Closed Christmas Day.
Phone:	(706) 866–9241, ext. 123
Web site:	http://www.nps.gov/chch/index.htm
Description and comments:	If you are a Civil War buff, then this is a great stop for you. Some of the largest battles of the Civil War were fought in the hills surrounding this park; the object was to gain control

of Chattanooga, a key railroad hub and gateway to the Confederacy. Chickamauga Battlefield features a 7-mile self-guided auto tour, monuments, hiking trails, and horse trails. The visitor center contains a bookstore, presents information about the battles, and shows a 26-minute movie, *The Battle of Chickamauga.* We enjoyed viewing and learning about the different authentic cannons displayed outside the visitor center.

Exit 348

McDonald's with an Indoor Play Area

Driving time: 1 minute

Directions: Take exit 348 (GA-151/Ringgold/LaFayette) and go east 0.1 mile. McDonald's is on the right.

Exit 333

McDonald's with an Indoor Play Area

Driving time: 1 minute

Directions: Take exit 333 (GA-52/Walnut Avenue/Dalton) and go east 0.2 mile. McDonald's is on the right.

Georgia Mile Marker 320

Rest Area (*southbound only*)

This rest area has public restrooms, telephones, vending machines, picnic areas, and space for the kids to run.

Exit 312

McDonald's with an Indoor Play Area

Driving time:	1 minute
Directions:	Take exit 312 (GA-53/Calhoun/Fairmont) and go west 0.4 mile. McDonald's is on the left.

Georgia Mile Marker 308

Rest Area (*northbound only*)

This rest area has public restrooms, telephones, vending machines, picnic areas, and space for the kids to run.

Exit 293

Weinman Mineral Museum

Driving time:	2 minutes
Ages:	8 and up
Length of visit:	1–2 hours
Address:	51 Mineral Museum Drive, White, GA 30184
Directions:	Take exit 293 (US 411/Chattsworth/White) and go west 0.2 mile. Turn left on Mineral Museum Drive.
Cost:	$4 adults $3.50 seniors (ages 55 and up) $3 children (ages 6–11) Free for children under 6
Hours:	Mon–Sat 10 a.m.–5 p.m. Closed New Year's Day, Easter, Memorial Day, July 4, Labor Day, Thanksgiving Day, Christmas Eve, and Christmas Day.

Phone:	(770) 386-0576
Web site:	http://www.weinmanmuseum.org/
Description and comments:	If you and your family are interested in rocks and minerals, this is the museum for you. You will also find Indian artifacts and fossils. Kids can touch replicas of fossils and try panning for gold. The museum emphasizes the importance of minerals in the state of Georgia, which has a rich mining history and was the site of the first major gold rush in the nation.

Exit 290

McDonald's with an Outdoor Play Area

Driving time:	1 minute
Directions:	Take exit 290 (GA-20/Rome/Canton) and go east 0.2 mile. McDonald's is on the left.

Exit 288

Etowah Indian Mounds Historic Site

Driving time:	11 minutes
Ages:	10 and up
Length of visit:	2 hours
Address:	813 Indian Mounds Road SW Cartersville, GA 30120
Directions:	Take exit 288 (GA-113/Cartersville/Main Street) and head west. Follow GA-113 South signs for 3 miles. Go straight on Etowah Drive (GA-113 turns to the right at this point). Stay on Etowah Drive for 2.6 miles, to the entrance of the park.

Cost:	$4 adults $3.50 seniors (ages 65 and up) $2.50 children (ages 6–18) Free for children under 6
Hours:	Tue–Sat 9 a.m.–5 p.m., Sun 2 p.m.–5:30 p.m. Closed Thanksgiving Day, Christmas Day, and New Years Day.
Phone:	(770) 387-3747
Web site:	http://www.gastateparks.org/
Description and comments:	Visit this 54-acre site of mound-building Native Americans who lived between A.D. 1000 and A.D. 1550. Here you will find burial mounds, a village area, and a defensive ditch. See the 63-foot flat-topped knoll that was used as a platform for the home of the priest-chief. In another mound, nobility were buried in elaborate costumes along with items they would need in the afterlife. Visit the museum, where you will see numerous Native American artifacts, including an 8,000-year-old bowl that was found in a local farmer's field.

Exit 285

Red Top Mountain State Park

Driving time:	5 minutes
Ages:	All
Length of visit:	1–3 hours
Address:	50 Lodge Road SE, Cartersville, GA 30121
Directions:	Take exit 285 (Red Top Mountain Road) and head east 2 miles to Red Top Mountain State Park visitor center.

The swimming beach at Red Top Mountain State Park

Cost:	$3 per vehicle
Hours:	7 a.m.–10 p.m.
Phone:	(770) 975–0055
Web site:	http://www.gastateparks.org/
Description and comments:	Red Top Mountain State Park is a 1,428-acre park on Lake Allatoona. You will notice that even the drive to the park is beautiful. As you drive across the lake on the bridge, you get a panoramic view of the water and the surrounding area. Wildlife abounds (especially deer—be careful driving!) and is viewable from the roads and trails. The park has camping, cottages, and a 33-room lodge with a restaurant. Also in the park are a boat ramp, a marina, a swimming beach, a playground, and picnic areas. There are five trails between 0.75 mile and 5.5 miles in length. We especially enjoyed the Lakeside Trail, with a great view of the lake starting near the lodge. If you enjoy fishing, stop by the bait store at the gas station near I-75, and then fish from the pier just before the park entrance. This park is a great stop for nature lovers.

Kid Trivia

Red Top Mountain gets its name from the soil's red color, which is caused by high iron-ore content. This area was once an important iron-mining area.

Exit 277

McDonald's with an Outdoor Play Area

Driving time: 1 minute

Directions: Take exit 277 (GA-92) and go west 0.2 mile. McDonald's is on the left.

Exit 273

McDonald's with an Indoor Play Area
Burger King with an Outdoor Play Area
Southern Museum of Civil War and Locomotive History

McDonald's with an Indoor Play Area

Driving time: 1 minute

Directions: Take exit 273 (Wade Green Road/Kennesaw) and go east 0.5 mile. McDonald's is on the left.

Burger King with an Outdoor Play Area

Driving time: 1 minute

Directions: Take exit 273 (Wade Green Road/Kennesaw) and go east 0.5 mile. Burger King is on the right.

Southern Museum of Civil War and Locomotive History

Driving time:	5 minutes
Ages:	10 and up
Length of visit:	2 hours
Address:	2829 Cherokee Street, Kennesaw, GA 30144
Directions:	Take exit 273 (Wade Green Road/Kennesaw) and head west on Wade Green Road 3.4 miles (Wade Green Road becomes Cherokee Street). The Southern Museum of Civil War and Locomotive History is on the right, just before the railroad tracks.
Cost:	$7.50 adults $6.50 seniors (ages 60 and up) $5.50 children (ages 4–12) Free for children under 4
Hours:	Mon–Sat 9:30 a.m.–5 p.m., Sun noon–5 p.m. Closed New Year's Day, Easter, Thanksgiving Day, and Christmas Day.
Phone:	(770) 427-2117
Web site:	http://www.southernmuseum.org/
Description and comments:	Visit the museum that houses The General, the engine from the great locomotive chase during the Civil War. Northern raiders, trying to wreck the Confederate supply line between Atlanta and Chattanooga, stole The General. The Southerners recaptured the train after a dramatic 86-mile chase. The Walt Disney movie *The Great Locomotive Chase* is based on this incident. The museum depicts how railroads played a significant role in the Civil War, including their contributions to troop movement and hospital care. This museum, renovated in 2003, is a member of the prestigious Smithsonian Affiliations Program.

Georgia Trivia

- Georgia is the largest state east of the Mississippi.
- Georgia became a state in 1788. It was the fourth of the original 13 colonies.
- Georgia was named for King George II of England.
- Georgia is the nation's number one producer of the three Ps—peanuts, pecans, and peaches.

Exit 269

Kennesaw Mountain National Battlefield Park
Chick-Fil-A with an Indoor Play Area
Chuck E. Cheese
Burger King with an Outdoor Play Area
Town Center at Cobb Mall
McDonald's with an Outdoor Play Area

Kennesaw Mountain National Battlefield Park

Driving time:	8 minutes
Ages:	10 and up
Length of visit:	2 hours
Address:	900 Kennesaw Mountain Drive
Kennesaw, GA 30152
Directions:	Take exit 269 (to US 41/Barrett Parkway/Kennesaw) and head west 2.2 miles. Turn left on Old Highway 41 (not US 41) and go 1.4 miles. Turn right at the light onto Stilesboro Road. The park visitor center is immediately on the left. You can follow brown and white signs to the park from I-75.

Cost:	Park: Free
	Mountaintop bus rides: $2 adults
	$1 children (ages 6–12)
	Free for children under 6
Hours:	Park: Dawn–dusk
	Visitor center: 8:30 a.m.–5 p.m.
	Closed Thanksgiving Day, Christmas Day, and New Year's Day.
Phone:	(770) 427–4686
Web site:	http://www.nps.gov/kemo/index.htm
Description and comments:	Kennesaw Mountain Battlefield is a 2,888-acre national battlefield park commemorating the over 67,000 soldiers that were killed, wounded, or captured in the 1864 Atlanta campaign of the Civil War. Stop and get introductory information about the park and the battle at the visitor center. From there, explore any of the 16 miles of walking trails, where you will see cannons in their original positions and signs describing events from the battles. Take a hike on the trail 1.2 miles up to the top of Kennesaw Mountain from the visitor center. On weekends, take the shuttle bus that runs every half-hour to take you to the top of the mountain and back down again. The view from the top of the mountain is wonderful on a clear day. You can view downtown Atlanta to the south and the Red Top Mountain area to the north. During our visit, we found that many families love to visit this park to picnic or hike.

Chick-Fil-A with an Indoor Play Area

Driving time:	2 minutes
Directions:	Take exit 269 (to US 41/Barrett Parkway/Kennesaw) and go west 0.6 mile. Chick-Fil-A is on the right.
Comment:	Chick-Fil-A restaurants are closed on Sunday.

Chuck E. Cheese

Driving time:	2 minutes
Ages:	2–12
Length of visit:	1–2 hours
Address:	824 Ernest W. Barrett Parkway Kennesaw, GA 30144
Directions:	Take exit 269 (to US 41/Barrett Parkway/Kennesaw) and go west 0.7 mile. Chuck E. Cheese is on the right.
Cost:	Admission: Free Arcade tokens: $0.25 (all games one token)
Hours:	Sun–Thu 10 a.m.–10 p.m., Fri–Sat 10 a.m.–11 p.m.
Phone:	(770) 420–3340
Web site:	http://www.chuckecheese.com/
Description and comments:	Kids can play child-appropriate arcade games, crawl around in a climbing play area, or watch Chuck E. Cheese and his band play music. There's even a toddler zone with special games for the smallest players. If you get hungry, you can purchase pizza, sandwiches, and salads. This Chuck E. Cheese has a Kid Check program, in which a staff member stamps your group's hands for identification. To make sure kids leave with the group they came with, a staff member checks their hand stamps as they exit. We like going to Chuck E. Cheese for driving stops as they are generally clean, safe, and give the kids a fun place to blow off steam while their parents relax.

Burger King with an Outdoor Play Area

Driving time:	3 minutes
Directions:	Take exit 269 (to US 41/Barrett Parkway/Kennesaw) and head west 1.3 miles. Burger King is on the right.

Town Center at Cobb Mall

Driving time:	2 minutes
Ages:	All
Length of visit:	1 hour
Address:	400 Ernest W. Barrett Parkway NW Kennesaw, GA 30144
Directions:	Take exit 269 (to US 41/Barrett Parkway/Kennesaw) and go east 0.4 mile. The mall is on the left.
Cost:	Free
Hours:	Mon–Sat 10 a.m.–9 p.m., Sun noon–6 p.m.
Phone:	(770) 424–9486
Web site:	http://www.simon.com/
Description and comments:	Stop and take a driving break at the Town Center at Cobb Mall. This major mall has 220 stores, including JCPenney, Sears, Macy's, and Parisian. Small coin-operated rides and a food court are available.

McDonald's with an Outdoor Play Area

Driving time:	2 minutes
Directions:	Take exit 269 (to US 41/Barrett Parkway/Kennesaw) and go east 0.4 mile. McDonald's is on the right.

Atlanta Driving

If you are heading south, you are now approaching the Atlanta area. Interstate traffic is very heavy during rush hour and should be avoided if possible. Our experience is that rush hour in Atlanta is from about 6 a.m.–10 a.m. and 3 p.m.–7 p.m. on weekdays. It is best to plan accordingly. Be sure to read the ATMS (Advanced Traffic Management System) signs over I-75 for up-to-date traffic information. If you must drive through Atlanta during rush hour or if there are accidents on I-75, then taking the I-285 bypass west around Atlanta is usually a better choice. To take the bypass from I-75 heading south, take exit 259, (I-285W). You will rejoin I-75 south at mile 238.

Exit 265

American Adventures
Six Flags White Water

American Adventures

Driving time:	5 minutes
Ages:	2–12
Length of visit:	2–4 hours
Address:	250 Cobb Parkway North, Marietta, GA 30062
Directions:	Take exit 265 (GA-120/Marietta) and go east 0.4 mile. Turn right on Wallace Road and go 0.9 mile. Turn right on Cobb Parkway and go 0.3 mile. American Adventures and Six Flags White Water are on the right. You can follow signs from I-75.
Cost:	$15 guests 36 inches and over $5 children under 36 inches $5 parents with children Admission includes the Foam Factory, amusement park rides, and miniature golf.

Go-kart rides: $5

Parking: $6

Hours: Hours are variable, so call or see the Web site before you visit.

General hours:
March
Sat 10 a.m.–6 p.m., Sun noon–6 p.m.

April–late May
Sat 10 a.m.–6 p.m., Sun 11 a.m.–6 p.m.

Memorial Day weekend–early August
Daily 10 a.m.–8 p.m.

Mid-August–September
Sat 10 a.m.–6 p.m., Sun 11 a.m.–6p.m.

October
Sat 10 a.m.–6 p.m., Sun noon–6 p.m.

Closed November–February.

Phone: (770) 948–9290

Web site: http://www.sixflags.com/

Description and comments: American Adventures is geared for kids under 12 years old. This relatively small amusement park is perfect for youngsters not quite ready for big rides at the major amusement parks. Rides include a kid coaster, Tilt-A-Whirl, a rocking pirate ship, a giant slide, and a junior version of bumper cars. Miniature golf, an indoor arcade, and go-karts are also available. Kids will love playing at the Foam Factory, where they can launch foam balls at their favorite target (bull's-eyes, younger siblings, etc.) in the 40,000-square-foot indoor play area. If you get hungry, you can purchase corn dogs, pizza, chicken tenders, ice cream, and other goodies at the snack bar.

Six Flags White Water

Driving time: 5 minutes

Ages: 1 and up

Length of visit:	2–4 hours
Address:	250 Cobb Parkway North, Marietta, GA 30062
Directions:	Take exit 265 (GA-120/Marietta) and go east 0.4 mile. Turn right on Wallace Road and go 0.9 mile. Turn right on Cobb Parkway and go 0.3 mile. American Adventures and Six Flags White Water are on the right. You can follow signs from I-75.
Cost:	$31.99 $21.99 children under 48 inches tall Parking: $6
Hours:	Hours are variable, so call or see the Web site before you visit. General hours: Mid-May–Memorial Day Weekends 10 a.m.–6 p.m. Memorial Day–early August Daily 10 a.m.–8 p.m. Early August–Labor Day Weekends 10 a.m.–6 p.m. Closed mid-September–mid-May.
Phone:	(770) 948-9290
Web site:	http://www.sixflags.com/
Description and comments:	If you're driving near Atlanta during a hot summer day, stop by and enjoy a great water park. Toddlers and preschoolers will love playing in the three-story tree house or at Little Squirts Island, which includes fountains, squirt guns, chutes, and slides. Thrill seekers in your family should try the Tornado, where you swirl down a 132-foot tunnel, or the Cliffhanger, where you take a 90-foot freefall down the water slide. The less adventurous can stick to the wave pool, family slides, body flumes, the six-person raft ride, or the lazy river. Pizza, sandwiches, burgers, and plenty of cold treats are available.

Dave & Buster's

Driving time:	2 minutes
Ages:	3 and up
Length of visit:	1–2 hours
Address:	2215 D and B Drive SE, Marietta, GA 30067
Directions:	Take exit 261 (GA-280/Lockheed/Dobbins AFB) and go west 0.2 mile. Turn left on Franklin Road SE and go 0.2 mile. Turn left on Northwest Parkway and go 0.3 mile to Dave & Buster's.
Cost:	Admission: Free Purchase a debit card to play games. Expect to pay $1–$3 per game.
Hours:	Sun–Wed 11:30 a.m.–midnight, Thu 11:30 a.m.–1:00 a.m., Fri–Sat 11:30 a.m.–2:00 a.m.
Phone:	(770) 951-5554
Web site:	http://www.daveandbusters.com/
Description and comments:	Stop and play arcade games at Dave & Buster's. You'll also find many ride simulation games and activities like Skee-Ball. Food is available. This is a good place for kids to play in the daytime; however, in the late evening patrons are mostly adults. This Dave & Buster's is very crowded on weekend nights, especially Friday.

Start of I-285 Atlanta Bypass

Exit 10B (I-285)	

Six Flags Over Georgia

Driving time: 6 minutes from I-285

Ages: 3 and up

Length of visit: 2–5 hours

Address: 7561 Six Flags Parkway SW, Austell, GA 30168

Directions: Take I-285 exit 10B (I-20 west) and go 3 miles. Take I-20 exit 47 (Six Flags Parkway). Turn left on Six Flags Parkway. Parking is on the right.

Cost: $45.99
$29.99 children under 48 inches tall
$29.99 seniors (ages 55 and up)
Free for children under 2

Be sure to check the Web site for significant online specials.

Parking: $12

Ride Superman Ultimate Flight roller coaster
(Photo courtesy of Six Flags Over Georgia)

Hours:	Hours are variable, so call or see the Web site before you visit.
	General hours: March Weekends 10 a.m.–6 p.m.
	April–late May Sat 10 a.m.–10 p.m., Sun 10 a.m.–8 p.m.
	Memorial Day weekend–mid-June Mon–Fri 10 a.m.–6 p.m., Sat 10 a.m.–10 p.m., Sun 10 a.m.–8 p.m.
	Mid-June–mid-August Sun–Fri 10 a.m.–9 p.m., Sat 10 a.m.–10 p.m.
	Mid-August–October Sat 10 a.m.–8 p.m., Sun 10 a.m.–6 p.m.
	Closed November–February.
Phone:	(770) 948–9290
Web site:	http://www.sixflags.com/
Description and comments:	If you and your family enjoy major amusement parks, Six Flags Over Georgia is the place for you. There are plenty of rides for kids of all ages. Roller coaster enthusiasts will love the great selection of 10 coasters. Bugs Bunny World is an entire section of rides for kids less than 54 inches tall, complete with a soft play fort, bumper cars, a theater, and plenty of other rides and attractions for preschool- and school-age kids. During a hot summer day, be sure to visit Skull Island, which is a 1-acre water park inside Six Flags Over Georgia. The main feature is a 66-foot-high skull that dumps over 1,000 gallons of water over anyone daring enough to get under it. Kids also enjoy water wheels, sprayers, fountains, water slides, and bridges. Be sure to bring extra clothes. You'll find many places to eat inside the park.

Looking For a Hotel?

If you are looking for a hotel on the north side of the I-285 Atlanta bypass, look no further. We enjoy the Fairfield Inn & Suites just west of I-285 at GA exit 18. In general, we consider Fairfield Inn & Suites a good value. For under $70, we receive a nice room, access to an outdoor pool, and a continental breakfast. This hotel is a three (out of five) diamond AAA-rated hotel. Call (770) 435–4500 to speak to the hotel staff.

Exit 7 (I-285)

McDonald's with an Indoor Play Area

Driving time:　　1 minute from I-285

Directions:　　Take I-285 exit 7 (Cascade Road) and go west 0.4 mile to McDonald's.

Exit 60 (I-285)

McDonald's with an Outdoor Play Area

Driving time:　　2 minutes from I-285

Directions:　　Take I-285 exit 60 (GA-139) and go south 0.1 mile (note that I-285 travels east-west along this stretch). Turn left on Shoreham Drive and go 0.1 mile. Turn right on Heather Lane to McDonald's.

Returning to I-75

Exit 258
Chuck E. Cheese
Cumberland Mall

Chuck E. Cheese

Driving time: 4 minutes

Ages: 2–12

Length of visit: 1–2 hours

Address: 2990 Cumberland Boulevard SE
Atlanta, GA 30339

Directions: Take exit 258 (Cumberland Boulevard) and head west 1.5 miles. Chuck E. Cheese is on the left.

Cost: Admission: Free
Arcade tokens: $0.25 (all games one token)

Hours: Sun–Thu 10 a.m.–10 p.m.,
Fri–Sat 10 a.m.–11 p.m.

Phone: (770) 435–9036

Web site: http://www.chuckecheese.com/

Description and comments: Kids can play child-appropriate arcade games, crawl around in a climbing play area, or watch Chuck E. Cheese and his band play music. There's even a toddler zone with special games for the smallest players. If you get hungry, you can purchase pizza, sandwiches, and salads. This Chuck E. Cheese has a Kid Check program, in which a staff member stamps your group's hands for identification. To make sure kids leave with the group they came with, a staff member checks their hand stamps as they exit. We like going to Chuck E. Cheese for driving stops as they are generally clean, safe, and give the kids a fun place to blow off steam while their parents relax.

Cumberland Mall

Driving time:	3 minutes
Ages:	2 and up
Length of visit:	1 hour
Address:	1000 Cumberland Mall, Atlanta, GA 30339
Directions:	Take exit 258 (Cumberland Boulevard) and head west 1 mile. The Cumberland Mall is on the right.
Cost:	Free
Hours:	Mon–Sat 10 a.m.–9 p.m. Sun noon–6 p.m. Closed Thanksgiving Day and Christmas Day.
Phone:	(770) 435–2206
Web site:	http://www.cumberlandmall.com/
Description and comments:	Stretch your legs at this major mall. Anchor stores include JCPenney, Macy's, and Sears. An ample food court and small coin-operated rides are available. Note that this mall is undergoing a major renovation that should be completed by late 2006. The mall will continue to operate during the renovation.

Exit 255

McDonald's with an Indoor Play Area

Driving time:	1 minute
Directions:	Take exit 255 (Route 41/West Paces Ferry Road/Northside Parkway) and go east 0.1 mile. McDonald's is on the left.

Piedmont Park

Driving time:	7 minutes
Ages:	2 and up
Length of visit:	1–3 hours
Address:	400 Park Drive NE, Atlanta, GA 30306
Directions heading south:	Take exit 250 (10th–14th Streets/Techwood Drive). Go straight through the light at the end of the exit ramp, crossing 14th Street. Stay to the left when the road splits, and at the next light turn left on 10th Street. Go 0.6 mile and turn left on Piedmont Avenue. The Piedmont park community center is located a block ahead on the right (in the same building as Willie's Mexican Grill, just before 12th Street). A small parking lot is located behind the building. However, you may need to park on the street around the perimeter of the park as parking spaces are limited.
Directions heading north:	Take exit 250 (10th–14th Streets/GA Tech). Turn right on 10th Street and go 0.5 mile. Turn left on Piedmont Avenue. The Piedmont park community center is located a block ahead on the right (in the same building as Willie's Mexican Grill, just before 12th Street). A small parking lot is located behind the building. However, you may need to park on the street around the perimeter of the park as parking spaces are limited.
Cost:	Park: Free
	Pool: Free swim times Mon–Fri 1:30 p.m.–4:15 p.m.
	Other times $3 adults $1 children (ages 6–12) Free for children under 6

Hours:	Park: 6 a.m.–11 p.m.
	Pool: Memorial Day–Labor Day Mon–Fri 1:30 p.m.–7:30 p.m., Weekends noon–7:30 p.m.
Phone:	Park: (404) 875-7275 Pool: (404) 892-0117 Botanical Gardens: (404) 876-5859
Web site:	http://www.piedmontpark.org/
Description and comments:	This 190-acre park is a touch of serenity in the middle of Atlanta. Here you can enjoy miles of paved walking and running trails, two playgrounds, picnic tables, tennis courts, basketball courts, soccer fields, baseball fields, and roller-skating and biking areas. Most folks seem to come just to take pleasure in the beauty of the expansive hardwood trees and green space. Piedmont Park celebrated its 100-year anniversary in 2004. While here, you can learn about the park's rich history, which includes the South's first intercollegiate football game. If you have some extra time, stop at the Atlanta Botanical Garden adjacent to the park. Restrooms are available.

EXIT

Exit 249C or 248C

Imagine It! The Children's Museum of Atlanta
Centennial Olympic Park

Imagine It! The Children's Museum of Atlanta

Driving time:	8 minutes
Ages:	8 and under
Length of visit:	1–3 hours
Address:	275 Centennial Olympic Park Drive NW Atlanta, GA 30313

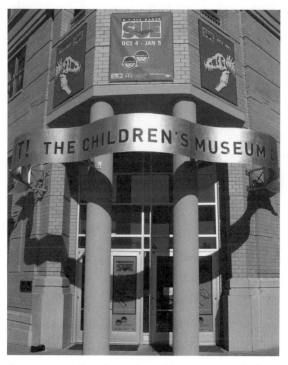

(Photo courtesy of Imagine It! The Children's Museum of Atlanta)

Directions heading south: Take exit 249C (Williams Street). Go straight off the exit to Williams Street and go 0.5 mile. Turn right on Baker Street. Use the Inforum parking lot immediately on the left. The museum is across Baker Street on the corner of Baker Street and Centennial Park Drive.

Directions heading north: Take exit 248C (GA-10/Andrew Young International Boulevard/Freedom Parkway/Carter Center). Veer right off the exit to stay on Andrew Young International Boulevard and go 0.8 mile. Turn right on Williams Street and go 0.3 mile. Turn left on Baker Street. Use the Inforum parking lot immediately on the left. The museum is across Baker Street on the corner of Baker Street and Centennial Park Drive.

Cost: $11

Free for children under 3

Parking: $5 with a museum ticket stub in the Inforum lot

This museum is a member of ACM.

Hours: Mon–Fri 10 a.m.–4 p.m.
Sat–Sun 10 a.m.–5 p.m.

Closed Thanksgiving Day and Christmas Day.

Phone: (404) 659-5437

Web site: http://www.imagineit-cma.org

Description and comments: If you have kids under 8 years old, this is a great place to stop. Imagine It! opened in 2003 and is designed for kids aged 2–8. There is plenty for kids to do, including tap dancing, dressing up, food packaging, and playing with ball machines and a sand table. The sand here is extra fun. It can be molded, so kids can make sandcastles and other shapes without the mess of wet sand. The food conveyor area is also popular. Here kids pack food in boxes, send it down the conveyor line, and start the process over again. Kids aged 5 and younger will like their own place with a water play area and a climbing treehouse. Also, youngsters under age 2 have an area just for them, complete with water tables, a train table, and blocks to enjoy. If you get hungry, enjoy a sandwich at the snack area.

Centennial Olympic Park

Driving time: 6 minutes

Ages: 2 and up

Length of visit: 1–2 hours

Address: 265 Marietta Street, Atlanta, GA 30313

Directions heading south:	Take exit 249C (Williams Street). Turn right on Alexander Street and go 0.8 mile. Turn left on Marietta Street and go 0.2 mile. Turn right into the Green parking lot. Walk across Marietta Street to Centennial Olympic Park. There is additional parking around the perimeter of the park.
Directions heading north:	Take exit 248C (GA-10/Andrew Young International Boulevard/Freedom Parkway/Carter Center). Turn left on Andrew Young International Boulevard and go 0.9 mile. Turn left on Centennial Olympic Park Drive and go 0.2 mile. Turn right on Marietta Street and follow signs to the Green parking lot. Walk across Marietta Street to Centennial Olympic Park. There is additional parking around the perimeter of the park.
Cost:	Park: Free Parking: $8 in the Green Lot
Hours:	7 a.m.–11 p.m.
Phone:	(404) 222-7275
Web site:	http://www.centennialpark.com/
Description and comments:	Stop by the world-famous park of the 1996 Olympic Games. Watch the water display, cool off in the Fountain of Rings in the heat of the summer (be sure to bring extra clothes), let the kids play in the playground, grab a bite to eat at the café, or just take a stroll among the relaxing water features. If you are lucky, you may catch some of the free entertainment that varies throughout the year, including midday, evening, and weekend concert series; Family Fun Days; the Fourth of July Celebration; and the Holiday in Lights festival, complete with an ice-skating rink. Call or see the Web site if you want to catch a specific activity.

Atlanta's New Attraction—The World's Largest Aquarium

Located a few blocks west of Imagine It! The Children's Museum of Atlanta, the Georgia Aquarium holds 8 million gallons of water and is home to more than 100,000 fish, including the only whale sharks on display outside of Asia. The aquarium is open Sunday–Thursday 9 a.m.–6 p.m. and Friday–Saturday 9 a.m.–8 p.m. Call (404) 581–4000 or visit http://www.georgiaaquarium.com for more information.

Exit 248A or 246

World of Coca-Cola

Driving time:	4 minutes
Ages:	5 and up
Length of visit:	1–2 hours
Address:	55 Martin Luther King Jr. Drive Atlanta, GA 30303
Directions heading south:	Take exit 248A (Martin Luther King Jr. Drive), and go 3 blocks. Parking is on the right, just before the World of Coca-Cola building.
Directions heading north:	Take exit 246 (Fulton Street/Central Avenue/Downtown). Go 0.7 mile and turn right on Mitchell Street. Go 0.1 mile and turn left on Capital Avenue. Go 0.1 mile and turn left on Martin Luther King Jr. Drive. Go 0.2 mile. Parking is on the right, just before the World of Coca-Cola building.
Cost:	$9 adults $8 seniors (ages 60 and up) $5 children (ages 4–11) Free for children under 4 Parking: $5

Hours:	September–May, Mon–Sat 9 a.m.–5 p.m., Sun 11 a.m.–5 p.m.
	June–August, Mon–Sat 9 a.m.–6 p.m., Sun 11 a.m.–5 p.m.
	Closed Easter, Thanksgiving Day, and Christmas Day. Closes at 3 p.m. on Christmas Eve and New Year's Eve.
Phone:	(800) 676-2653
Web site:	http://www.woccatlanta.com/
Description and comments:	This three-story museum pays tribute to Coca-Cola products. You can look inside huge Coke cans, where you can make soda bubbles, see Coca-Cola history videos, and hear old radio jingles. Kids enjoy "catching" Coca-Cola products in their cups in the Tastes of the States area. Also, you can taste drinks from around the world in Tastes of the World. (It's a good thing the bathrooms are located near these areas!) The World of Coca-Cola will be moving to a new complex sometime in 2007. The new location will be adjacent to Centennial Olympic Park, along with the Georgia Aquarium.

Got a few extra minutes?

If you have more time to spend in this area, take a walk from the World of Coca-Cola to Underground Atlanta (food and shopping), the CNN Center, or the Georgia State Capitol.

Exit 247

Zoo Atlanta

Driving time:	4 minutes
Ages:	All
Length of visit:	1–3 hours

Address: 800 Cherokee Avenue SE, Atlanta, GA 30315

Directions: Take exit 247 (I-20) and head east toward Augusta
                      1 mile. Take I-20 exit 59A. Turn right on Boule-
                      vard and go 0.5 mile. Zoo Atlanta parking is on
                      the right.

Cost: $17 adults
                      $13 seniors (ages 55 and up)
                      $12 children (ages 3–11)
                      Free for children under 3

                      Parking: Free

                      Norfolk Southern Zoo Express Train: $1.50

                      Nabisco Endangered Species Carousel: $1.50
                      Rock climbing: $3

Hours: 9:30 a.m.–4:30 p.m.

                      Closed Thanksgiving Day and Christmas Day.

                      This zoo is a member of AZA.

Phone: (404) 624–5600

Web site: http://www.zooatlanta.org/

Description and   This zoo's collection consists of over 700 speci-
comments: mens living in their natural environments. Check
                      out the reptiles, monkeys, otters, tigers, ele-
                      phants, birds, and many other animals. Be sure
                      to visit the fascinating displays of giant pandas,
                      gorillas, and orangutans. Youngsters will enjoy
                      the train ride, the carousel, petting the goats in
                      the children's zoo, and riding pretend animals
                      at the playground. There is even a rock-climbing
                      wall to conquer. The parking lots fill up quickly
                      on the weekends.

Elephant Artist

Starlet O'Hara, an African elephant at Zoo Atlanta, paints pictures. You
can purchase a painting by her for about $20. Her paintings have been
sold for as much as $1,800!

Exit 233

Southlake Mall

Driving time:	2 minutes
Ages:	2 and up
Length of visit:	1–2 hours
Address:	1000 Southlake Mall, Morrow, GA 30260
Directions:	Take exit 233 (GA-54/Morrow/Lake City) and go west 0.2 mile. Turn right on Southlake Parkway into the mall.
Cost:	Admission: Free
	Carousel rides: $1
Hours:	Mon–Sat 10 a.m.–9 p.m., Sun noon–6 p.m.
Phone:	(770) 961–1050
Web site:	http://www.southlakemall.com/
Description and comments:	Stop at Southlake Mall and stretch your legs before or after driving through Atlanta. Here you will find over 120 department stores and specialty shops including Macy's, JCPenney, Sears, American Eagle, and Victoria's Secret. Kids can ride on the carousel. Have lunch or dinner at the food court before you get back on I-75.

Exit 231

McDonald's with an Indoor Play Area

Driving time:	1 minute
Directions:	Take exit 231 (Mount Zion Boulevard) and go west 0.1 mile. Turn left on Mount Zion Parkway and go 0.1 mile to McDonald's.

Atlanta Driving

If you are heading north, you are now approaching the Atlanta area. Interstate traffic is very heavy during rush hour and should be avoided if possible. Our experience is that rush hour in Atlanta is from 6 a.m.–10 a.m. and 3 p.m.–7 p.m. on weekdays. It is best to plan accordingly. Be sure to read the ATMS (Advanced Traffic Management System) signs over I-75 for up-to-date traffic information. If you must drive through Atlanta during rush hour or if there are accidents on I-75, then taking the I-285 bypass west around Atlanta is usually a better choice. To take the bypass from heading north on I-75, take exit 238B (I-285W). You will rejoin I-75 north at mile 259.

Exit 221

McDonald's with an Indoor Play Area

Driving time: 1 minute

Directions: Take exit 221 (Jonesboro Road/Lovejoy) and go west 0.1 mile. McDonald's is on the left.

Exit 218

McDonald's with an Indoor Play Area
Burger King with an Outdoor Play Area

McDonald's with an Indoor Play Area

Driving time: 1 minute

Directions: Take exit 218 (GA-20/GA-81/McDonough/Hampton) and go east 0.3 mile. Turn right on Old Industrial Boulevard and go 0.1 mile to McDonald's.

Burger King with an Outdoor Play Area

Driving time: 1 minute

Directions: Take exit 218 (GA-20/GA-81/McDonough/ Hampton) and go east 0.2 mile. Burger King is on the left.

Exit 212

McDonald's with an Indoor Play Area

Driving time: 1 minute

Directions: Take exit 212 (Locus Grove/Hampton) and go east 0.1 mile. McDonald's is on the right.

Exit 198

High Falls State Park

Driving time: 3 minutes

Ages: All

Length of visit: 2 hours

Address: 76 High Falls Park Drive, Jackson, GA 30233

Directions: Take exit 198 (High Falls Road) and head east 1.8 miles. High Falls State Park is on the left.

Cost: $3 per vehicle

Pool: $4

Miniature golf: $2

Hours: Park: 7 a.m.–10 p.m.

Park office: 8 a.m.–5 p.m.

Pool: Memorial Day–Labor Day
Wed–Fri 11 a.m.–6 p.m.,
Weekends 11 a.m.–7 p.m.

Phone:	(478) 993–3053
Web site:	http://www.gastateparks.org/
Description and comments:	This 1,050-acre state park is great for a quick rest break or for a longer stay. We watched ducks swim in the 650-acre lake and were mesmerized by the Towaliga River waterfalls near the entrance of the park. Our kids enjoyed playing on the huge rocks, finding pine cones, and playing on the small, sand-based, plastic outdoor playground. The park also has seasonal swimming in the outdoor pool as well as miniature golf. You can picnic at one of the five picnic shelters, canoe in High Falls Lake (visit the park office for prices and availability), or take a walk along the 4.5 miles of trails. This is a great place to unwind after driving south through Atlanta.

Exit 187

McDonald's with an Outdoor Play Area

Driving time:	2 minutes
Directions:	Take exit 187 (GA-83/Forsyth/Monticello) and go west 0.2 mile. Turn right on GA-42 and go 0.1 mile to McDonald's.

Georgia Mile Marker 179

Rest Area (*southbound only*)

This rest area has public restrooms, telephones, picnic areas, vending machines, space for kids to run, and tourist information.

Start of I-475 Macon Bypass

> ## Why Take the I-475 Macon Bypass?
>
> I-75 travels east to Macon and then back west. The I-475 bypass travels almost straight north and south. I-475 takes you from I-75 exit 177 to I-75 exit 156 in only 15 miles, compared to 19 miles on I-75. Also, I-475 is less congested than I-75 and has many fun family stops along the way.

Exit 9 (I-475)

McDonald's with an Indoor Play Area
Chick-Fil-A with an Indoor Play Area
The Museum of Arts and Sciences

McDonald's with an Indoor Play Area

Driving time: 1 minute from I-475

Directions: Take I-475 exit 9 (Zebulon Road) and go east 0.2 mile. McDonald's is on the right.

Chick-Fil-A with an Indoor Play Area

Driving time: 1 minute from I-475

Directions: Take I-475 exit 9 (Zebulon Road) and go east 0.5 mile. Chick-Fil-A is on the right.

Comment: Chick-Fil-A restaurants are closed on Sunday.

The Museum of Arts and Sciences

Driving time:	10 minutes from I-475
Ages:	2 and up
Length of visit:	1–2 hours
Address:	4182 Forsyth Road, Macon, GA 31210
Directions:	Take I-475 exit 9 (Zebulon Road) and head east 2.5 miles until Zebulon Road ends at US 41/GA-19. Turn right on US 41/GA-19 and go 2 miles. Turn right into the Museum of Arts and Sciences parking lot (0.2 mile past the railroad viaduct).
Cost:	$7 adults $6 seniors (ages 62 and up) $5 students (ages 12 and up) $4 children (ages 2–11) Free for children under 2 This museum is a member of ASTC.
Hours:	Mon 9 a.m.–8 p.m., Tue–Sat 9 a.m.–5 p.m., Sun 1 p.m.–5 p.m. Closed New Year's Day, Easter, Memorial Day, July 4, Labor Day, Thanksgiving Day, Christmas Eve, and Christmas Day.
Phone:	(478) 477–3232
Web site:	http://www.masmacon.com/
Description and comments:	This museum has a unique combination of animals, art, and child-focused exhibits. Take a walk through the two-story tree house where kids can watch small monkeys, reptiles, and other animals. Kids can also view fossils, play with giant Lego blocks, and play in an art studio. Grownups may enjoy the changing, short-term art exhibits. We liked watching birds and squirrels eat from an outdoor feeder through the aviary window.

Georgia Mile Marker 8 (I-475)

Rest Area (*northbound only*)

This rest area has public restrooms, telephones, picnic areas, and vending machines. We enjoy walking along the paved trails through the oak and pine forest at this rest area.

Exit 5 (I-475)
Chuck E. Cheese
Colonial Mall Macon
Olympia Family Fun Center

Chuck E. Cheese

Driving time:	5 minutes from I-475
Ages:	2–12
Length of visit:	1–2 hours
Address:	3374 Mercer University Drive, Macon, GA 31204
Directions:	Take I-475 exit 5 (GA-74/Macon/Thomaston) and head east 2.8 miles. Chuck E. Cheese is on the right.
Cost:	Admission: Free Arcade tokens: $0.25 (all games one token)
Hours:	Sun–Thu 10 a.m.–10 p.m., Fri–Sat 10 a.m.–11 p.m.
Phone:	(478) 755-0915
Web site:	http://www.chuckecheese.com/
Description and comments:	Kids can play child-appropriate arcade games, crawl around in a climbing play area, or watch Chuck E. Cheese and his band play music. There's even a toddler zone with special games for the smallest players. If you get hungry, you

can purchase pizza, sandwiches, and salads. This Chuck E. Cheese has a Kid Check program, in which a staff member stamps your group's hands for identification. To make sure kids leave with the group they came with, a staff member checks their hand stamps as they exit. We like going to Chuck E. Cheese for driving stops as they are generally clean, safe, and give the kids a fun place to blow off steam while their parents relax.

Colonial Mall Macon

Driving time:	5 minutes from I-475
Ages:	All
Length of visit:	1–2 hours
Address:	3661 Eisenhower Parkway, Macon, GA 31206
Directions:	Take I-475 exit 5 (GA-74/Macon/Thomaston) and head east 2.3 miles. The mall is on the right.
Cost:	Admission: Free Carousel rides: $1
Hours:	Mon–Sat 10 a.m.–9 p.m., Sun noon–6 p.m.
Phone:	(478) 477–8840
Web site:	http://www.colonialmallmacon.com/
Description and comments:	Colonial Mall Macon offers 200 specialty shops, Belk, Macy's, JCPenney, Sears, Parisian, and Dillard's. Enjoy the carousel (which has a spinning teacup older children will enjoy) and a large arcade with both family and adult games. You'll find plenty of food choices at the two-story food court.

Olympia Family Fun Center

Driving time:	1 minute from I-475
Ages:	4 and up
Length of visit:	1–2 hours
Address:	5020 Mercer University Drive, Macon, GA 31210
Directions:	Take I-475 exit 5 (GA-74/Macon/Thomaston) and go east 0.3 miles. The Olympia Family Fun Center is on the right.
Cost:	Skating: $7
Hours:	This center operates primarily when school is out (evenings, weekends, and summer), but hours are variable. Visit the Web site or call for current hours.
Phone:	(478) 474–0747
Web site:	http://www.olympiaskate.com/
Description and comments:	This center has roller-skating, laser tag, an arcade, and outdoor batting cages. Concessions are available.

Returning to I-75

Exit 149
McDonald's with an Outdoor Play Area
Burger King with an Outdoor Play Area

McDonald's with an Outdoor Play Area

Driving time:	1 minute
Directions:	Take exit 149 (GA-49/Byron/Fort Valley) and go east 0.2 mile. McDonald's is on the right.
Comment:	This outdoor play area is larger than most.

Burger King with an Outdoor Play Area

Driving time: 1 minute

Directions: Take exit 149 (GA-49/Byron/Fort Valley) and go east 0.2 mile. Burger King is on the left.

Comment: This outdoor play area is larger than most.

Exit 136

McDonald's with an Indoor Play Area
Burger King with an Outdoor Play Area
Chick-Fil-A with an Indoor Play Area

McDonald's with an Indoor Play Area

Driving time: 2 minutes

Directions: Take exit 136 (US 341/Perry/Fort Valley), and go east 0.3 mile. McDonald's is on the right.

Burger King with an Outdoor Play Area

Driving time: 1 minute

Directions: Take exit 136 (US 341/Perry/Fort Valley) and go east 0.1 mile. Burger King is on the left.

Chick-Fil-A with an Indoor Play Area

Driving time: 2 minutes

Directions: Take exit 136 (US 341/Perry/Fort Valley) and go east 0.5 mile. Chick-Fil-A is on the right.

Comment: Chick-Fil-A restaurants are closed on Sunday.

Georgia Mile Marker 118

Rest Area (*southbound only*)

This rest area has public restrooms, telephones, picnic areas, vending machines, and space for kids to run.

Kid Trivia

Look at the peanuts growing in the fields just west of mile marker 115. About half of all the peanuts in the United States are grown in Georgia. Peanuts are unusual plants because they flower above ground, but bear fruit underground. The shelled peanut is the seed, which is planted in April or May and grows into an oval-leafed plant about 18 inches tall. Peanuts are harvested in September or October. The peanut is actually not a nut at all. It's a legume, just like peas and beans.

Georgia Mile Marker 108

Rest Area (*northbound only*)

This rest area has public restrooms, telephones, picnic areas, vending machines, and space for kids to run.

Exit 101

McDonald's with an Indoor Play Area
Burger King with an Outdoor Play Area

McDonald's with an Indoor Play Area

Driving time: 1 minute

Directions: Take exit 101 (US 280/GA-30/GA-90/Cordele/ Abbeville) and go west 0.3 mile. McDonald's is on the right.

Are you nuts?

More pecans are grown in Georgia than in any other state. See if you can find pecan orchards just west of I-75 between mile markers 105 and 101.

Burger King with an Outdoor Play Area

Driving time: 3 minutes

Directions: Take exit 101 (US 280/GA-30/GA-90/Cordele/ Abbeville) and go west 0.9 mile. Burger King is on the right.

Kid Trivia

Look for cotton fields near mile markers 115 and 100. You'll see cotton bolls in late fall and early winter. Cotton is the soft fiber that grows around the seeds of the cotton plant. Georgia produces enough cotton in one year to make about 350 million pairs of jeans.

Georgia Mile Marker 85

Rest Area (*northbound only*)

This rest area has public restrooms, telephones, picnic areas, and vending machines. We enjoy the scenic walking trails along the pine trees at this rest area.

Exit 82

McDonald's with an Outdoor Play Area

Driving time: 1 minute

Directions: Take exit 82 (GA-107/GA-112/Ashburn/Fitzger-ald) and go west 0.2 mile. McDonald's is on the left.

Georgia Mile Marker 76

Rest Area (*southbound only*)

This rest area has public restrooms, telephones, picnic areas, vend-ing machines, and space for kids to run.

Exit 63B

Georgia Agrirama

Driving time:	2 minutes
Ages:	8 and up
Length of visit:	1–2 hours
Address:	1492 Whiddon Mill Road, Tifton, GA 31793
Directions:	Take exit 63B and go west 0.3 mile. Turn right on Agrirama drive. Stop at the Tourist Information Center to get tickets.
Cost:	$7 adults $6 seniors (ages 55 and up) $4 children (ages 5–16) Free for children under 5
Hours:	Tue–Sat 9 a.m.–5 p.m. Closed New Year's Day, Labor Day, Thanksgiving Eve, Thanksgiving Day, and December 19th–26th.
Phone:	(800) 767–1875

Logging train at the Georgia Agrirama (Photo courtesy the Georgia Agrirama)

Web site:	http://www.agrirama.com/
Description and comments:	The Georgia Agrirama is the state's living history center. You will find restored and preserved farm communities, an industrial area, and a rural town from the late 1800s on this 95-acre complex. Costumed interpreters are on location daily to explain and demonstrate the lifestyles and activities. Kids can explore the farms and see ham and bacon being cured, visit barnyard animals (no touching), and take a train ride through the woods. Stroll down Main Street and see how consumers shopped over 100 years ago. Snacks and ice cream can be purchased. The Agrirama is best suited for school-age kids and adults who are interested in agricultural history.

EXIT

Exit 63A

Burger King with an Outdoor Play Area
Fulwood Park
McDonald's with an Indoor Play Area

Burger King with an Outdoor Play Area

Driving time:	1 minute
Directions:	Take exit 63A (2nd Street) and go east 0.1 mile. Burger King is on the right.

Fulwood Park

Driving time:	6 minutes
Ages:	2 and up
Length of visit:	1–2 hours
Directions:	Take exit 63A (2nd Street) and head east 1.4 miles. Turn left on Tift Avenue. Fulwood Park is on the right, just past 8th Street.

Cost:	Free
Hours:	Dawn–dusk
Description and comments:	Take a driving break and enjoy the serenity of this 28-acre community park. Fulwood Park features picnic areas, restrooms, a playground, and wooded areas with large hardwood trees.

McDonald's with an Indoor Play Area

Driving time:	2 minutes
Directions:	Take exit 63A (2nd Street) and go east 0.2 mile. McDonald's is on the right.

Exit 62

Wendy's with an Indoor Play Area
Chick-Fil-A with an Outdoor Play Area
Paradise Public Fishing Area

Wendy's with an Indoor Play Area

Driving time:	2 minutes
Directions:	Take exit 62 (US 82/US 319/Sylvester) and go west 0.3 mile. Wendy's is on the left.

Chick-Fil-A with an Outdoor Play Area

Driving time:	1 minute
Directions:	Take exit 62 (US 82/US 319/Sylvester) and go west 0.1 mile. Chick-Fil-A is on the right.
Comment:	Chick-Fil-A restaurants are closed on Sunday.

Paradise Public Fishing Area

Driving time:	15 minutes
Ages:	4 and up
Length of visit:	1–4 hours
Directions:	Take exit 62 (US 82/US 319/Sylvester) and head east 9 miles. Turn right at Whitley Road and go 0.1 mile. Turn left on County Road 406 (Brookville-Nashville Road) and then left into the Paradise Public Fishing Area entrance. Directions are signed from US 82.
Cost:	Admission: Free
	Fishing licenses are required for those over 16 years old.
Hours:	Dawn–dusk
Phone:	(229) 533–4792
Description and comments:	If you want to go fishing or view wildlife and you have some time to spare, Paradise Public Fishing Area is a great place to visit. The area features freshwater fishing, with 60 lakes and ponds and many fishing piers. During our last visit, many anglers were trying their luck off the banks as well as in boats. Although managed primarily for public fishing, this is also a great place to view wildlife. Numerous species of birds, mammals, snakes (including rattlesnakes—we have never seen any, but be careful anyway), and tortoises are found here. Bald eagles visit the area from October to mid-March. You can also see osprey, hawks, geese, and ducks. Public restrooms are available.

Georgia Mile Marker 48

Rest Area

This rest area has public restrooms, telephones, picnic areas, vending machines, and space for kids to run.

Exit 39

McDonald's with an Indoor Play Area
Burger King with an Outdoor Play Area
Reed Bingham State Park

McDonald's with an Indoor Play Area

Driving time: 1 minute

Directions: Take exit 39 (GA-37/Adel/Moultrie) and go east
                     0.2 mile. McDonald's is on the left.

Burger King with an Outdoor Play Area

Driving time: 2 minutes

Directions: Take exit 39 (GA-37/Adel/Moultrie) and go west
                 0.1 mile. Take the first left turn and go 0.2 mile to
                 Burger King (in the King Frog factory store area).

Reed Bingham State Park

Driving time: 8 minutes

Ages: All

Length of visit: 1–4 hours

Address: 542 Reed Bingham Road, Adel, GA 31620

Directions:	Take exit 39 (GA-37/Adel/Moultrie) and head west 5.6 miles. Turn right on Evergreen Church Road and go 0.4 mile. Turn left on Reed Bingham Road and go 0.5 mile to the entrance of the park.
Cost:	$3 per vehicle
Hours:	Park: 7 a.m.–10 p.m.
	Park office: 8 a.m.–5 p.m.
Phone:	(229) 896-3551
Web site:	http://www.gastateparks.org/
Description and comments:	This 1,600-acre park has a scenic lake with plenty of fishing (try your luck around the dam) and boating activity. Relax on the well-maintained sandy beach as the kids swim in the lake (no lifeguards are present). Or have a picnic, take a walk on the trails, and let the kids expend some energy at the outdoor playground. Nature lovers may be able to spot waterfowl and tortoises. The most famous visitors may be the thousands of vultures that drop in from late November through early April. Reed Bingham State Park was a pleasant surprise for us and a great place for a family stop.

Exit 22

Burger King with an Indoor Play Area and Attached Dairy Queen

Driving time:	1 minute
Directions:	Take exit 22 (US 41S/North Valdosta Road) and go west 0.1 mile. Burger King is on the right.

Exit 18

McDonald's with an Outdoor Play Area
Chick-Fil-A with an Indoor Play Area
Burger King with an Outdoor Play Area
Colonial Mall Valdosta

McDonald's with an Outdoor Play Area

Driving time: 2 minutes

Directions: Take exit 18 (GA-133/Valdosta/Moultrie) and go east 0.6 mile. McDonald's is on the left.

Chick-Fil-A with an Indoor Play Area

Driving time: 2 minutes

Directions: Take exit 18 (GA-133/Valdosta/Moultrie) and go east 0.6 mile. Chick-Fil-A is on the right.

Comment: Chick-Fil-A restaurants are closed on Sunday.

Burger King with an Outdoor Play Area

Driving time: 1 minute

Directions: Take exit 18 (GA-133/Valdosta/Moultrie) and go east 0.4 mile. Burger King is on the right.

Colonial Mall Valdosta

Driving time: 2 minutes

Ages: All

Length of visit: 1–2 hours

Address: 1700 Norman Drive, Valdosta, GA 31601

Directions:	Take exit 18 (GA-133/Valdosta/Moultrie) and go east 0.4 mile. Turn left into the mall entrance.
Cost:	Free
Hours:	Mon–Sat 10 a.m.–9 p.m., Sun 1 p.m.–6 p.m.
Phone:	(229) 242-0457
Web site:	http://www.colonialmallvaldosta.com/
Description and comments:	Visit Colonial Mall Valdosta, with major stores including Belk, Sears, and JCPenney. You can also enjoy a carousel and a large arcade with family and adult games. The food court here is smaller than at most malls but has all the standard items, such as subs, burgers, pizza, a Chick-Fil-A, Chinese food, and cookies.

Exit 16

McDonald's with an Outdoor Play Area

Driving time:	2 minutes
Directions:	Take exit 16, (US 84/GA-94/US 221/Valdosta/Quitman), and go east 0.5 mile. McDonald's is on the left.

Exit 13

Wild Adventures

Driving time:	6 minutes
Ages:	2 and up
Length of visit:	2–5 hours

Address: 3766 Old Clyattville Road
Valdosta, GA 31601

Directions: Take exit 13 (Valdosta/Old Clyattville Road) and head west on Old Clyattville Road 4 miles. Wild Adventures is on the right.

Cost: $39.95 adults
$34.95 seniors (ages 55 and up)
$34.95 children (ages 3–9)
Free for children under 3

Parking: $7

Hours: The park opens at 10 a.m. most days and has variable closing times. Call, check the Web site, or tune in to 92.1 FM on the radio for current operating hours.

Closed Easter, Thanksgiving Day, Christmas Eve, and Christmas Day.

Web site: http://www.wild-adventure.com/

Splash Island at Wild Adventures

Going to Wild Adventures?

If you are within 40 miles of Valdosta, the best source of information is 92.1 FM on the radio. This is the Wild Adventures radio station. The station gives continuous park information, including operating hours.

Phone: (229) 219-7080

Description and comments: This is a great amusement park for families. With over 55 rides, there are plenty for kids of all ages, including nine roller coasters, family thrill rides, water rides, and plenty of smaller rides for toddlers and preschoolers. As advertised, the lines here do seem shorter than at other amusement parks. On a hot summer day, be sure to bring a swimsuit and enjoy the very popular Splash Island. Splash Island is a park in itself, complete with a rain fortress, lazy river, and fast water slides. Toddlers and preschoolers will love the area with smaller water slides and waterfalls. Wild Adventures started out as an animal park: animal lovers can enjoy viewing giraffes, elephants, zebras, kangaroos, wallabies, emus, and other animals. Choose from four indoor restaurants to satisfy your appetite before you get back on the highway.

Exit 5

Chick-Fil-A with an Indoor Play Area
McDonald's with an Outdoor Play Area

Chick-Fil-A with an Indoor Play Area

Driving time: 2 minutes

Directions: Take exit 5 (GA-376/Lakes Boulevard) and go east 0.5 mile. Chick-Fil-A is on the left.

Comment: Chick-Fil-A restaurants are closed on Sunday.

McDonald's with an Outdoor Play Area

Driving time: 1 minute

Directions: Take exit 5 (GA-376/Lakes Boulevard) and head
west. Turn right at the first light. McDonald's is
on the right.

Georgia Mile Marker 3

Georgia Welcome Center (*northbound only*)

This welcome center has public restrooms, telephones, picnic areas,
vending machines, tourist information, and space for kids to run.
Be sure to pick up a free coupon book if you are planning to stop at
a hotel in Georgia.

CHAPTER
S E V E N

Florida

Top Florida Family Stops

O'Leno State Park
Florida Museum of Natural History
Paynes Prairie Preserve State Park
Silver Springs/Wild Waters Waterpark
Orlando Science Center

Florida Quick View

Attraction	Florida Exit Number
Zoo or Aquarium	None
Park	439, 414, 374
Museum	384, 341, 265 (Turnpike)
Mall	427, 387, 350, 267B (Turnpike)
Family Entertainment Center	267B (Turnpike)
Rest Area Mile Marker	470 (southbound only), 445 (southbound only), 442 (northbound only), 411, 382, 346, 301 (Turnpike), 264 (Turnpike)
Fast Food with an Indoor Play Area	427, 384, 267B (Turnpike), 259 (Turnpike)
Fast Food with an Outdoor Play Area	427, 399, 387, 384, 350, 267B (Turnpike)
Other Attraction	352, 254 (Turnpike)

Florida Emergency Information

Emergency Phone:	911
Florida Highway Patrol Cell:	*FHP (*347)
Exits with Police Sign:	none
Exits with Hospital Sign:	387, 384

Florida Mile Marker 470

Florida Welcome Center (*southbound only*)

This welcome center has public restrooms, telephones, picnic areas, visitor information, vending machines, and space for kids to run.

Florida Mile Marker 445

Rest Area (*southbound only*)

This rest area has public restrooms, telephones, vending machines, picnic areas, and space for kids to run.

Florida Mile Marker 442

Rest Area (*northbound only*)

This rest area has public restrooms, telephones, vending machines, picnic areas, and space for kids to run.

Exit 439

Stephen Foster Folk Culture Center State Park

Driving time:	5 minutes
Ages:	2 and up
Length of visit:	1–2 hours
Address:	US Highway 41 North, White Springs, FL 32096
Directions:	Take exit 439 (SR 136) and head east 3 miles. Turn left on US 41 to the entrance of Stephen Foster Folk Culture Center State Park.
Cost:	$4 per vehicle

Hours:	Park: 8 a.m.–dusk
	Museum and gift shop: 9 a.m.–5 p.m.
Phone:	(386) 397–4331
Web site:	http://www.floridastateparks.org/
Description and comments:	This park honors the memory of Stephen Foster, who wrote the songs "Oh Susanna," "Camptown Races," and "Old Folks at Home" (better known as the "Suwannee River" song). You can visit the Stephen Foster Museum, walk or bike on the trails, fish in the Suwannee River, or enjoy the beauty of this 650-acre park. Many families relax among the scenic forest oaks while the kids play on the playground. This is a great park for a picnic.

Florida Call Boxes

Call boxes are located at 1-mile increments along I-75 in Florida. Travelers can use these to summon help for vehicle problems or if they need medical or police help. When a call box is activated, it sends the request to the nearest Florida Highway Patrol operator, who dispatches the appropriate assistance.

Exit 427

McDonald's with an Indoor Play Area
Burger King with an Outdoor Play Area
Lake City Mall

McDonald's with an Indoor Play Area

Driving time:	1 minute
Directions:	Take exit 427 (US 90/Lake City/Live Oak) and go east 0.4 mile. McDonald's is on the left.

Burger King with an Outdoor Play Area

Driving time:	1 minute
Directions:	Take exit 427 (US 90/Lake City/Live Oak) and go east 0.3 mile. Burger King is on the right.

Lake City Mall

Driving time:	4 minutes
Ages:	2 and up
Length of visit:	1 hour
Address:	2469 West US Highway 90, Lake City, FL 32055
Directions:	Take exit 427 (US 90/Lake City/Live Oak) and head east 1 mile. Lake City Mall is on the left.
Cost:	Free
Hours:	Mon–Sat 10 a.m.–9 p.m., Sun 12:30 p.m.–5:30 p.m.
Phone:	(386) 755-4848.
Web site	http://www.shoplakecitymall.com/
Description and comments:	Stop and stretch your legs at the Lake City Mall. Here you will find stores such as JCPenney and Belk, along with small coin-operated rides, a snack area, and a Chinese food restaurant. There is no food court. This mall is smaller than most.

Looking for a Hotel?

On multiple occasions, we have stayed at the Lake City Country Inn & Suites, just west of FL exit 427. For under $120 (Internet rate), we receive a king suite, access to a heated indoor pool, and a continental breakfast. We really enjoy the king suite as the adults sleep in the king-size bed and the kids sleep on the sofa bed in the separate living room. This hotel is a three (out of five) diamond AAA-rated hotel. Call (386) 754-5944 to speak to hotel staff.

O'Leno State Park

Driving time:	8 minutes
Ages:	2 and up
Length of visit:	1–4 hours
Address:	410 SE O'Leno Park Road, High Springs, FL 32643
Directions:	Take exit 414 (US 41/US 441/Lake City/High Springs) and head west off the exit. Go south on US 41/US 441 for 6 miles. Turn left on Sprite Road to the O'Leno State Park entrance.
Cost:	$4 per vehicle Canoe rental: $3 per hour
Hours:	8 a.m.–dusk
Phone:	(386) 454–1853
Web site:	http://www.floridastateparks.org/

Ths Santa Fe River at O'Leno State Park

Description and comments:	If you want to relax and enjoy the outdoors, then this 6,000-acre state park is a great place to stop. O'Leno State Park has many scenic walking trails, including the River Trail and the Limestone Trail. Try to find alligators (rare) or turtles along the River Trail as you walk along the Santa Fe River to the "river sink," where the river disappears underground. The Limestone Trail passes through beautiful hardwood trees and then by a pine forest. These trails are well maintained and marked. Kids can play on the playground located near the picnic area. You can also swim in the river at the designated swimming area, but there is no lifeguard on duty. During our visit, many families were swimming, fishing, picnicking, and enjoying the outdoors.

Florida Trivia

- Orange juice is the official state beverage.
- Florida became the 27th state in 1845.

Florida Mile Marker 411

Rest Area

This rest area has public restrooms, telephones, a picnic area, vending machines, and space for kids to run.

Exit 399

McDonald's with an Outdoor Play Area

Driving time:	1 minute
Directions:	Take exit 399 (FL-441/Alachua/High Springs) and go east 0.1 mile. McDonald's is on the right.

Exit 387

McDonald's with an Outdoor Play Area
The Oaks Mall

McDonald's with an Outdoor Play Area

Driving time: 2 minutes

Directions: Take exit 387 (FL-26/Gainseville/Newberry) and
go east 0.6 mile. McDonald's is on the right.

The Oaks Mall

Driving time: 2 minutes

Ages: All

Length of visit: 1–2 hours

Address: 6419 Newberry Road, Gainesville, FL 32605

Directions: Take exit 387 (FL-26/Gainseville/Newberry), and
go east 0.3 mile. The Oaks Mall is on the right.

Cost: Free

Hours: Mon–Sat 10 a.m.–9 p.m.,
Sun noon–6 p.m.

Phone: (352) 331-4411

Web site: http://www.theoaksmall.com/

Description and   Stop and unwind at The Oaks Mall. This is a
comments: major mall with over 140 stores, including Sears,
Belk, Macy's, JCPenney, and Dillard's. You can
enjoy a large food court, a soft play area for kids
less than 42 inches tall, and an arcade for the
bigger kids.

Exit 384
Chick-Fil-A with an Indoor Play Area McDonald's with an Outdoor Play Area Florida Museum of Natural History

Chick-Fil-A with an Indoor Play Area

Driving time: 1 minute

Directions: Take exit 384 (FL-24/Gainesville/Archer) and go east 0.4 mile. Chick-Fil-A is on the right.

Comment: Chick-Fil-A restaurants are closed on Sunday.

McDonald's with an Outdoor Play Area

Driving time: 1 minute

Directions: Take exit 384 (FL-24/Gainesville/Archer) and go east 0.1 mile. McDonald's is on the left.

Florida Museum of Natural History

Driving time: 5 minutes

Ages: 8 and up

Length of visit: 2 hours

Address: SW 34th Street and Hull Road
Gainesville, FL 32611

Directions: Take exit 384 (FL-24/Gainesville/Archer) and head east 1.4 miles. Turn left on SW 34th Street. At the third light, turn right on Hull Road and go 0.2 mile. The entrance to the Florida Museum of Natural History is on the right. Directions are signed from I-75.

Cost:	Free ($6 per person donation suggested)
	Butterfly Rainforest:
	$7.50 adults
	$6.50 seniors (ages 62 and up)
	$6.50 students (ages 13 and up)
	$4.50 children (ages 3–12)
	Free for children under 3
	Parking: $3 weekdays, free weekends
	This museum is a member of ASTC.
Hours:	Mon–Sat 10 a.m.–5 p.m.,
	Sundays and holidays 1 p.m.–5 p.m.
	Closed Thanksgiving Day and Christmas Day.
Phone:	(352) 846–2000
Web site:	http://www.flmnh.ufl.edu/
Description and comments:	Located on the campus of the University of Florida, this is the largest natural history museum in the Southeast. Visitors can see a life-size limestone replica of a cave and a 14-foot-tall mammoth skeleton. We enjoyed viewing ancient shark jaws (the Megaladon jaw is enormous) as well as looking at miniature sea life through a microscope. There is plenty of Florida natural history to enjoy for the whole family. For an additional fee, enjoy the tranquility of numerous waterfalls and over 55 species of butterflies fluttering overhead at the Butterfly Rainforest.

Gatorade Is from Gators

In 1967, a University of Florida research team developed a drink to replace fluids and help prevent dehydration and heat illnesses, such as muscle cramping and heat exhaustion, in athletes. Members of the Florida Gators football team were the first test subjects. This drink became known as "Gatorade."

Florida Mile Marker 382

Rest Area

This rest area has public restrooms, telephones, picnic areas, vending machines, and space for kids to run.

Exit 374

Paynes Prairie Preserve State Park

Driving time:	5 minutes
Ages:	3 and up
Length of visit:	1–3 hours
Address:	100 Savannah Boulevard, Micanopy, FL 32667
Directions:	Take exit 374 (CR–234/Micanopy) and head east 1.4 miles. Turn left on US 441 and go 0.6 mile. Turn right on Savanna Boulevard to the entrance of Paynes Prairie Preserve State Park.
Cost:	$4 per vehicle
Hours:	8 a.m.–dusk
Phone:	(352) 466–3397
Web site:	http://www.floridastateparks.org/
Description and comments:	Paynes Prairie Preserve is a 21,000-acre secluded wilderness where bison and wild horses roam freely. The preserve offers more than 30 miles of hiking, horseback riding, and bicycling trails. Try your luck fishing at Wauberg Lake. Enjoy a picnic (grills and picnic tables are provided) while the kids play on the playground. Be sure to stop at the visitor center to get oriented to this massive preserve.

View from the glass-bottom boat ride at Silver Springs
(Printed by permission of Silver Springs)

Exit 352

Silver Springs
Wild Waters Waterpark

Silver Springs

Driving time:	15 minutes
Ages:	2 and up
Length of visit:	1–3 hours
Address:	5656 East Silver Springs Boulevard Silver Springs, FL 34488
Directions:	Take exit 352 (SR 40/Ocala/Silver Springs) and head east 9 miles. Silver Springs is on the right.
Cost:	$32.99 adults $29.99 seniors (ages 55 and up) $23.99 children (ages 3–10) Free for children under 3

Combination tickets, Silver Springs and Wild Waters Waterpark:

$35.99 adults

$32.99 seniors (ages 55 and up)

$26.99 children (ages 3–10)

Free for children under 3

Parking: $6

Hours: 10 a.m.–5 p.m.

Phone: (352) 236–2121

Web site: http://www.silversprings.com/

Description and comments: Located at the headwaters of the Silver River, these springs gush nearly 550 million gallons of crystal clear water every day. This creates the largest natural artesian spring formation in the world. The waters of Silver Springs and the nearby Silver River are so transparent that this has become a favorite location for filming underwater scenes in movies and television shows. We enjoyed the glass-bottom boat ride (there are three different boat rides), on which we could see fish and turtles swimming below us. We also liked the fountain and light show as well as the 80-foot-tall lighthouse ride. Kids under 48 inches tall will like the Kids Ahoy area, with small rides (a carousel, boats, a Ferris wheel), a ball pit, and a climbing area. Animal lovers should enjoy viewing the bears, panthers, alligators, birds, and animal shows. Plenty of food and gift shops are available.

Silver Screen

The six original Tarzan movies, starring Johnny Weissmuller, were filmed at Silver Springs in the 1930s and 1940s. Also, *The Creature From the Black Lagoon* was filmed here in 1954.

Wild Waters Waterpark

Driving time:	15 minutes
Ages:	All
Length of visit:	2–4 hours
Address:	5656 East Silver Spring Boulevard Silver Springs, FL 34488
Directions:	Take exit 352 (SR 40/Ocala/Silver Springs) and head east 9 miles. Wild Waters Waterpark is on the right, next to Silver Springs.
Cost:	$23.99 adults $20.99 children shorter than 48 inches Free for children under 3 Combination tickets Silver Springs and Wild Waters Waterpark: $35.99 adults $32.99 seniors (ages 55 and up) $26.99 children (ages 3–10) Free for children under 3 Parking: $6
Hours:	Hours are variable, so call or see the Web site before you visit. General hours: Mid-April–late May, weekends 10 a.m.–5 p.m. Labor Day weekend–July, daily 10 a.m.–6 p.m. August–mid-September, weekends 10 a.m.–5 p.m.
Phone:	(352) 236–2121
Web site:	http://www.wildwaterspark.com/
Description and comments:	For families who enjoy water parks, this is a good one. Big kids can ride several thrilling water slides, like the 220-foot-long Silver Bullet. Kids can play in an area with water cannons, water valves, slides, and a swing bridge. The wave pool, with 4-foot waves, is very popular. Preschoolers and toddlers will enjoy the wading area, complete with fountains and water animals.

EXIT

Exit 350

Chick-Fil-A with an Outdoor Play Area
Burger King with an Outdoor Play Area
Paddock Mall

Chick-Fil-A with an Outdoor Play Area

Driving time:	1 minute
Directions:	Take exit 350 (FL-200/Hernando/Dunnellon) and go east 0.2 mile. Chick-Fil-A is on the right.
Comment:	Chick-Fil-A restaurants are closed on Sunday.

Burger King with an Outdoor Play Area

Driving time:	1 minute
Directions:	Take exit 350 (FL-200/Hernando/Dunnellon) and go west 0.1 mile. Burger King is on the right.

Paddock Mall

Driving time:	3 minutes
Ages:	2 and up
Length of visit:	1–2 hours
Address:	3100 College Road, Ocala, FL 34474
Directions:	Take exit 350 (FL-200/Hernando/Dunnellon) and go east 0.8 mile. Paddock Mall is on the right.
Cost:	Free
Hours:	Mon–Sat 10 a.m.–9 p.m., Sun noon–5:30 p.m.
Phone:	(352) 237–1221

Web site:	http://www.simon.com/
Description and comments:	Take a driving break at Paddock Mall. Anchor stores include Belk, Macy's, JCPenney, and Sears. You'll also find over 90 stores, a food court, small coin-operated rides, and an arcade.

Florida Mile Marker 346

Rest Area

This rest area has public restrooms, telephones, a picnic area, vending machines, and space for kids to run.

Exit 341

Don Garlits Museum of Drag Racing

Driving time:	3 minutes
Ages:	8 and up
Length of visit:	1–3 hours
Address:	13700 SW 16th Avenue, Ocala, FL 34473
Directions:	Take exit 341 (CR–484/Belleview/Dunnellton) and go east 0.4 mile. Turn right on CR–475A and go 0.2 mile. The Don Garlits Museum of Drag Racing is on the right.
Cost:	$12 adults $10 seniors (ages 60 and above) $10 students (ages 13–18) $3 children (ages 5–12) Free for children under 5
Hours:	9 a.m.–5 p.m. Closed Christmas Day.

One of "Big Daddy's" famous dragsters

Phone:	(877) 271-3278
Web site:	http://www.garlits.com/
Description and comments:	Visit both of the museums in this complex. The Museum of Drag Racing displays over 150 cars and engines, including many of Don "Big Daddy" Garlits's famous dragsters. The second museum is the Museum of Antiques and Classic Cars, which displays an incredible collection of classic cars. Car buffs can literally spend all day at these two museums. For any drag racing fan or classic car fan, this is a great place to stop.

Start of Florida Turnpike

Florida Turnpike Mile Marker 301

Okahumpka Service Plaza

This service plaza has restrooms, a small arcade, a gas station, Popeyes Chicken, Dunkin' Donuts, TCBY, and Hot Dog City.

EXIT

Florida Turnpike Exit 267B

Chuck E. Cheese
West Oaks Mall
Chick-Fil-A with an Indoor Play Area
Burger King with an Indoor Play Area
TropiGrill with an Outdoor Play Area

Chuck E. Cheese

Driving time:	5 minutes from the turnpike
Ages:	2–12
Length of visit:	1–2 hours
Address:	7456 West Colonial Drive, Orlando, FL 32818
Directions:	Take Turnpike exit 267B (SR 50 to Orlando/Ocoee). Head east on Colonial Drive 4.2 miles. Chuck E. Cheese is on the right.
Cost:	Admission: Free Arcade tokens: $0.25 (all games one token)
Hours:	Sun–Thu 9 a.m.–10 p.m., Fri–Sat 9 a.m.–11 p.m.
Phone:	(407) 521-5997
Web site:	http://www.chuckecheese.com/
Description and comments:	Kids can play child-appropriate arcade games, crawl around in a climbing play area, or watch Chuck E. Cheese and his band play music. There's even a toddler zone with special games for the smallest players. If you get hungry, you can purchase pizza, sandwiches, and salads. This Chuck E. Cheese has a Kid Check program, in which a staff member stamps your group's hands for identification. To make sure kids leave with the group they came with, a staff member checks their hand stamps as they exit. We like going to

Chuck E. Cheese for driving stops as they are generally clean, safe, and give the kids a fun place to blow off steam while their parents relax.

Florida Oranges

Check out the orange groves near turnpike mile marker 277 on the west side. You'll see ripe oranges in late fall or early winter.

Florida produces about 80 percent of the oranges consumed in the United States. About 98 percent of these oranges are picked by hand. (Bet you can't think of a word that rhymes with orange!)

West Oaks Mall

Driving time:	5 minutes from the turnpike
Ages:	All
Length of visit:	1–2 hours
Address:	9401 West Colonial Drive, Ocoee, FL 34761
Directions:	Take Turnpike exit 267B (SR 50 to Orlando/ Ocoee). Head east on Colonial Drive 2.3 miles. West Oaks Mall is on the left.
Cost:	Free
Hours:	Mon–Sat 10 a.m.–9 p.m., Sun 11 a.m.–6 p.m.
Phone:	(407) 294-2775
Web site:	http://www.westoaksmall.com/
Description and comments:	Visit this major shopping mall, with over 120 stores, including Dillard's, Sears, and JCPenney. Families can enjoy the large food court, an arcade, small coin-operated rides, a carousel, and a soft play area just for toddlers and preschoolers.

Chick-Fil-A with an Indoor Play Area

Driving time:	2 minutes from the turnpike
Directions:	Take turnpike exit 267B (SR 50 to Orlando/ Ocoee). Head east on Colonial Drive 1.2 miles. Chick-Fil-A is on the right.
Comment:	Chick-Fil-A restaurants are closed on Sunday.

Burger King with an Indoor Play Area

Driving time:	4 minutes from the turnpike
Directions:	Take turnpike exit 267B (SR 50 to Orlando/ Ocoee). Head east on Colonial Drive 2.8 miles. Burger King is on the left.

TropiGrill with an Outdoor Play Area

Driving time:	5 minutes from the turnpike
Directions:	Take turnpike exit 267B (SR 50 to Orlando/ Ocoee). Head east on Colonial Drive 3.9 miles. TropiGrill is on the left.
Comment:	This restaurant serves fast-food type chicken.

Florida Turnpike Exit 265

Orlando Science Center

Driving time:	15 minutes from the turnpike
Ages:	All
Length of visit:	2–5 hours
Address:	777 East Princeton Street, Orlando, FL 32803

Directions: Take turnpike exit 265 (SR 408 toll road) east toward Orlando and Titusville. Head east on SR 408 for 9 miles. Take I-4 east (toward Daytona Beach) and go 3 miles. Take I-4 exit 85 (Princeton Street). Turn right on East Princeton Street and go 0.4 mile. Orlando Science Center is on the left. Parking is across the street.

Cost: $14.95 adults
$13.95 seniors (ages 55 and up)
$13.95 students with ID
$9.95 children (ages 3–11)
Free for kids under 3

The price includes admission to all exhibit galleries, giant-screen films, and planetarium shows.

Parking: $3.50 per day

This museum is a member of ASTC.

Learning about the body in Body Zone (Courtesy of Orlando Science Center)

Hours:	Mon–Thu 9 a.m.–5 p.m., Fri–Sat 9 a.m.–9 p.m., Sun noon–5 p.m.
Phone:	(888) 672–4386
Web site:	http://www.osc.org/
Description and comments:	This museum is one of the best we've visited, with something fun for every age, including parents. So even if your family is in town primarily for a theme park vacation, we highly recommend you find some time to visit this gem. There are many areas to visit. KidsTown is for kids under 48 inches tall and their parents. Young children will love to pick oranges from trees and send them to a packing plant or pretend they are driving a rocket ship. There is a small water-play area and a bubble-making area inside a kid-size house. There is also a small area where kids can play with trains. NatureWorks is the centerpiece (literally) of the museum. It's a 7,000 square-foot exhibit of Florida's diverse ecosystems, with a large open pond with fish and turtles and an adjoining area with aquariums and snakes. The Measure Me area was a hit with our whole family (even Mom and Dad). Here you can measure your size, strength, flexibility, balance, speed, and even the size of your foot. Then you can compare your "numbers" with all the visitors of the museum. Our kids loved to discover that Mommy's foot was larger than 80 percent of the other Mommies' feet. DinoDigs has large skeletons of several dinosaurs and a small area for children to dig up bones. In BodyZone you can see how your heart pumps blood and where your food goes, test your muscles, and build a skeleton. At Cosmic Tourist you can learn more about our solar system, roll balls in a large vortex, learn how it feels to be in an earthquake (on a moving platform), or see how tornadoes are formed. Other exhibits

include Science City which includes Physics Park, Power Station, 123 Math Avenue, and Light Power. The CineDome houses an eight-story domed movie screen and a large telescope, where you can observe the moon and planets during special (usually weekend) evening events.

Florida Turnpike Mile Marker 264

Turkeylake Service Plaza

This service plaza has restrooms, a small arcade, a gas station, Sbarro, Burger King, TCBY, and Starbucks.

Florida Turnpike Exit 259

McDonald's with Their Largest Indoor Play Area in the United States

Driving time:	4 minutes from the turnpike
Directions:	Take turnpike exit 259 (I-4 west). Take I-4 exit 74A (Sand Lake Drive) and go east 0.1 mile. McDonald's is on the left.
Comment:	Many play area activities cost money.

Florida Turnpike Exit 254

Gatorland

Driving time:	15 minutes from the turnpike
Ages:	3 and up

Length of visit:	2–4 hours
Address:	14501 South Orange Blossom Trail Orlando, FL 32837
Directions:	Take turnpike exit 254 (Orange Blossom Trail). Follow the sign toward Kissimmee and head south on 441/Orange Blossom Trail 5.7 miles. Gatorland is on the left.
Cost:	$19.95 adults (ages 13 and up) $9.95 children (ages 3–12) Free for children under 3 Parking: Free Train ride: $2 Hot dogs (alligator food): $2.50 Petting zoo food: $2
Hours:	9 a.m.–5 p.m.
Phone:	(800) 393-5297
Web site:	http://www.gatorland.com/
Description and comments:	As its name implies, this is a great place if you want to see alligators. The real attraction, at least for the kids, is watching the alligators jump almost five feet in the air to eat whole chickens in one of the daily shows (the gators were not quite so active when we were there on a cold December afternoon). Our kids enjoyed feeding the alligators hot dogs, but watch out for the aggressive birds. You can also take the Gatorland Express train, see other reptiles and birds, play on the mulch-based outdoor playground, and feed animals in the petting zoo.

Hotel Chain Toll-Free Numbers

AmeriHost Inn	(800) 434–5800
AmeriSuites	(877) 774–6467
Baymont Inn	(866) 999–1111
Best Western	(800) 780–7234
Budget Host Inn	(800) 283–4678
Budgetel Inn	(866) 999–1111
Clarion Suites	(877) 424–6423
Comfort Inn/Comfort Suites	(877) 424–6423
Country Hearth Inn	(800) 848–5767
Country Inn & Suites	(888) 201–1746
Courtyard By Marriott	(888) 236–2427
Days Inn	(800) 329–7466
Econo Lodge	(877) 424–6423
Fairfield Inn/ Fairfield Inn & Suites	(888) 236–2427
Hampton Inn	(800) 426–7866
Hilton	(800) 445–8667
Holiday Inn	(800) 465–4329
Holiday Inn Express	(800) 465–4324
Homewood Suites	(800) 225–5466
Howard Johnson	(800) 446–4656
Hyatt	(800) 633–7313

Knights Inn	(800) 843–5644
La Quinta Inn	(800) 531–5900
MainStay Suites	(877) 424–6423
Marriott	(888) 236–2427
Motel 6	(800) 466–8356
Quality Inn/ Quality Inn & Suites	(877) 424–6423
Ramada Inn/Ramada Limited	(800) 272–6232
Red Roof Inn	(800) 733–7663
Residence Inn	(888) 236–2427
Rodeway Inn	(877) 424–6423
Sheraton	(888) 625–5144
Shoney's Inn	(800) 552–4667
Signature Inn	(800) 822–5252
Sleep Inn	(877) 424–6423
Super 8 Motel	(800) 800–8000
Travelodge	(800) 578–7878
Wingate Inn	(800) 228–1000
Wyndham	(877) 999–3223

APPENDIX B

Car Travel Games

Use the car games listed below to help pass the time and maybe even learn a thing or two. All you need to play these games is an imagination.

Road Math

See who can add up all the numbers on a license plate. For example, if the license plate is 419XWQ, the players add the numbers 4 + 1 + 9 = 14. See who can find the highest total. See who can add the numbers on a license plate the quickest. If you have any multipliers in the car, see who can multiply license plate numbers together.

Cloud Animals

This tried-and-true outdoor game can also be played from inside the car on a partly cloudy day. Have someone in the car find a cloud in the sky that looks like a shape or an animal, and have him or her describe it. See who else can find that cloud.

Tebahpla (Alphabet Backwards)

See who can recite the alphabet backward. For kids that can do this easily, see how fast they can do it.

Animal Alphabet

See if the kids can name animals that begin with each letter of the alphabet. Begin with the letter *A*. For example, "*A* is for antelope." The game almost always ends with zebra.

Gross Sandwich

See who can describe the grossest sandwich. How about a peanut butter, fish, and mustard sandwich? Or a bacon, raw egg, and jelly wrap?

Number Slumber

Have someone pick a number. Then see how many words everyone can come up with that rhyme with that number. For example, four: door, store, bore, more, pour.

"If I Were Stranded on a Deserted Island . . ."

Imagine that you and your family are stranded on a deserted island. Ask each person what three items of food he or she would want to bring. Next, ask each person what three items he or she would want from home. You can create many versions of the game by asking about specific items. For example, you could ask what three toys, games, videos, books, music, clothes, or friends each person would want on the island.

J Is for Job

Encourage each passenger to think of a job that begins with a letter of the alphabet. The first player begins with the letter *A*, the second player *B*, and so on until you get through the alphabet. A slight twist is for someone to say a letter and then everyone tries to think of as many jobs as he or she can that begin with that letter.

Space Journey

Take an imaginary journey through outer space. Start at the sun and travel to Pluto. Take turns talking about each planet as you fly by each one. What is it like there? Is it hot or cold? Cloudy? Rocky? Are there any moons or rings? Just to help, here are the planets in order starting from the sun: Mercury, Venus, Earth, Mars, Jupiter, Saturn, Uranus, Neptune, and Pluto. Some interesting facts about planets in our solar system: Mercury is just a little larger than our moon, Venus is the hottest planet, Mars has the largest volcano, Jupiter is bigger than all the other planets put together, Saturn's rings are made of millions of chunks of ice, Uranus has at least 21 moons, Neptune has rings but they're smaller than Saturn's, and Pluto is the smallest planet and is smaller than our moon.

Mouth Mayhem

Have each passenger count his or her teeth—using their tongue. Each tooth counts as one point. You get two points for each missing tooth. Who has the most points? Who has the least points?

Vehicle Colors

Have each player choose a color. Whenever a player sees a vehicle of his or her chosen color, that player scores a point. The first player to score 25 points wins.

My Favorite Things

This game is a family favorite because you can learn a lot about each other while playing. Take turns stating a topic. Each person names his or her favorite item in that category. For example, the first person says, "Pizza toppings. My favorite pizza topping is sausage." Then each passenger shares his or her favorite pizza topping. Then someone else picks a different topic. This game goes on until you run out of topics.

The Opposite Game

Have the kids give the opposite of a word that you give them. For example: *over* and *under*, *long* and *short*, or *big* and *small*. Who is the tallest in the car? Who is the shortest? Who is the youngest? Who is the oldest?

Alphabet Search?

As a team, look for items that begin with each letter of the alphabet, starting with the letter *A* and continuing through *Z*. You can look inside the car or outside. (Hint: look for "Quick Lube" and "zoo" if you get stuck on *Q* and *Z*.)

States and Capitals

Give the players the name of a state and have them tell you the capital of that state. The player with the most correct answers wins. You can also reverse the game by giving the players the capital and having them tell you the state to which it belongs. Use the table below for reference.

State	Capital	State	Capital
Alabama	Montgomery	Louisiana	Baton Rouge
Alaska	Juneau	Maine	Augusta
Arizona	Phoenix	Maryland	Annapolis
Arkansas	Little Rock	Massachusetts	Boston
California	Sacramento	Michigan	Lansing
Colorado	Denver	Minnesota	St. Paul
Connecticut	Hartford	Mississippi	Jackson
Delaware	Dover	Missouri	Jefferson City
Florida	Tallahassee	Montana	Helena
Georgia	Atlanta	Nebraska	Lincoln
Hawaii	Honolulu	Nevada	Carson City
Idaho	Boise	New Hampshire	Concord
Illinois	Springfield	New Jersey	Trenton
Indiana	Indianapolis	New Mexico	Santa Fe
Iowa	Des Moines	New York	Albany
Kansas	Topeka	North Carolina	Raleigh
Kentucky	Frankfort	North Dakota	Bismarck

State	Capital	State	Capital
Ohio	Columbus	Texas	Austin
Oklahoma	Oklahoma City	Utah	Salt Lake City
Oregon	Salem	Vermont	Montpelier
Pennsylvania	Harrisburg	Virginia	Richmond
Rhode Island	Providence	Washington	Olympia
South Carolina	Columbia	West Virginia	Charleston
South Dakota	Pierre	Wisconsin	Madison
Tennessee	Nashville	Wyoming	Cheyenne

Help Us Write the Next Edition

Please help us make the next edition of *Parents' Survival Guide to I-75: Over 101 Fun Family Stops between Detroit and Orlando* even more useful to you. We would enjoy receiving feedback about what you liked about this book or ways to improve it. We would also like to receive information on any fun family stops along I-75 that your family enjoys. We will visit these places and may incorporate them into the next edition. Keep in mind that everything in this book is within 15 minutes from I-75 (or I-285 west bypassing Atlanta, I-475 bypassing Macon, or the Florida Turnpike along the way to Orlando). Please use the form below to record your information. Thank you!

Your name _____

Address _____

City _____ State _____ Zip _____

Phone _____ E-mail _____

My recommendation, change, or new place to visit:

Facility name _____ Phone number _____

State _____ Exit number _____

Directions _____

_____

Recommendation, change, or information on new facility:

_____

_____

Mail to: Majestic Palm Press
          PO Box 241
          Union, KY 41091

Fax to: (208) 460–8928

Index

About The Authors

After graduating from college, Daryl and Jacqueline West-field settled near Cincinnati, Ohio. Over the past 15 years they have driven over 30,000 miles on I-75 to visit family members in northern Ohio and central and southern Florida. More recently, with the help of their children, Mitchell and Alexandra, they performed extensive research to find fun family activities on I-75.